# Essential Series

Also in this series

John Cowell
Essential Visual Basic 4.0 fast
3-540-19998-5

John Cowell
Essential Delphi 2.0 fast
3-540-76026-1

John Cowell
Essential Java fast
3-540-76052-0

John Cowell
Essential Visual Basic 5.0 fast
3-540-76148-9

Duncan Reed and Peter Thomas
Essential HTML fast
3-540-76199-3

John Cowell
Essential Delphi 3 fast
3-540-76150-0

John Vince
Essential Virtual Reality fast
3-540-76124-1

# Springer

*London*
*Berlin*
*Heidelberg*
*New York*
*Barcelona*
*Budapest*
*Hong Kong*
*Milan*
*Paris*
*Santa Clara*
*Singapore*
*Tokyo*

John Hunt

# Essential JavaBeans *fast*

Springer

John Hunt, BSc, PhD, MBCS, CEng
Department of Computer Science, University of Wales, Aberystwyth, Dyfed,
Wales, SY23 3DB

*Series Editor*

John Cowell, BSc (Hons), MPhil, PhD
Department of Computer and Information Sciences, De Montfort
University, Kents Hill Campus, Hammerwood Gate, Kents Hill, Milton
Keynes, MK7 6HP, UK

ISBN 1-85233-032-5 Springer-Verlag Berlin Heidelberg New York

British Library Cataloguing in Publication Data
Hunt, John Edward
    Essential JavaBeans fast. - (Essential series)
    1.JavaBeans (Computer file) 2.Java (Computer program language)
    I.Title
    005.7'1262
    ISBN 1852330325

Library of Congress Cataloging-in-Publication Data
Hunt,John, 1946-
    Essential Javabeans fast / John Hunt.
        p.   cm. -- (Essential series)
    Includes index.
    ISBN 1-85233-032-5
    1. Java (Computer program language)  2. JavaBeans.   I. Title.
    II. Series: Essential series (Springer-Verlag)
    QA76.73.J38H85  1998
    005.13'3--dc21                                              98-7023

Typesetting: from author's postscript files
Printed and bound by the Creative Print & Design Group (Wales), Ebbw Vale
34/3830-543210 Printed on acid-free paper

*To my Godsons, Andrew and Euan.*

# Acknowledgements

I would like to thank the various students to whom I have taught JavaBeans. They unknowingly tested the notes on which this book is based. Many of them provided useful comments and feedback that were directly incorporated into this book. In particular, my thanks go to Matthew White and Liz Osbourne.

As always, I am hugely indebted to my wife Denise Cooke for her support and encouragement (as well as for her willingness to proof-read yet another Java book!).

*John Hunt*
*May 1998*

# Trademarks

Java, JDBC, Java Development Kit, Solaris, JavaBeans and Beans Development Kit are trademarks of Sun Microsystems, Inc. ActiveX, COM, DCOM and Windows 95 are registered trademarks of Microsoft Corporation. Unix is a registered trademark of AT&T. All other brand names are trademarks of their respective holders.

# Contents

Acknowledgements ........................................................................... vii

## 1 Introduction to JavaBeans ................................................ 1
Introduction ............................................................... 1
Objectives ................................................................. 1
Is this book for you? ..................................................... 2
How to use this book ..................................................... 2
Why have software components? ....................................... 2
What are JavaBeans? ..................................................... 3
JavaBeans and other component models ............................. 4
The JavaBeans package .................................................. 5
Bean terminology ......................................................... 5
Builder tool support ...................................................... 6
Building an application ................................................... 6
What you need to use JavaBeans ...................................... 7
How to get the BDK ...................................................... 8
What you get in the BDK ................................................ 9
Program conventions ..................................................... 11

## 2 Using the BeanBox ....................................................... 13
Introduction ............................................................... 13
Objectives ................................................................. 13
Starting the BeanBox .................................................... 14
The BeanBox .............................................................. 14
TheBeanBox menus ...................................................... 19
Working with Beans ...................................................... 20
Connecting Beans together .............................................. 24
Adding Beans to the BeanBox ......................................... 28
Builder tools ............................................................... 28

## 3 The Delegation Event Model ........................................... 29
Introduction ............................................................... 29
Objectives ................................................................. 29
Background ................................................................ 30
What is an event? ......................................................... 30
Delegating responsibility for an event ................................. 31
Event listeners ............................................................ 34
Working with events ...................................................... 34

Creating new events .............................................................. 36
Defining new listener interfaces .......................................... 37
Multicast and unicast sources ............................................. 39
Events and Beans ................................................................ 40

**4 Building Basic Beans** .......................................................... **41**
Introduction ......................................................................... 41
Objectives ........................................................................... 41
The JavaBeans architecture ............................................... 41
Creating a bean ................................................................... 42
The Beans conventions ....................................................... 42
The `BeanInfo` object .......................................................... 45
The `Counter` and `Alarm` beans ....................................... 45
Packaging the beans ............................................................ 50
Using the beans ................................................................... 51
JavaBeans and you ............................................................. 52

**5 Property Data Types** ............................................................ **55**
Introduction ......................................................................... 55
Objectives ........................................................................... 55
Simple properties ................................................................. 55
Bound properties ................................................................. 56
Constrained properties ........................................................ 62
Indexed properties ............................................................... 64

**6 Reflection and Bean Introspection** ..................................... **65**
Introduction ......................................................................... 65
Objectives ........................................................................... 65
Reflection ............................................................................. 66
The introspection process ................................................... 67
How it actually works ........................................................... 68
Experimenting with introspection ........................................ 69

**7 `BeanInfo` Objects** ............................................................... **71**
Introduction ......................................................................... 71
Objectives ........................................................................... 71
The `java.beans` package ................................................... 71
`BeanInfo` objects ............................................................... 72
The `BeanInfo` interface ...................................................... 72
Classes used with `BeanInfo` .............................................. 74
The `SimpleBeanInfo` class ................................................ 79
`AdditionalInfo` objects ....................................................... 79

The `getBeanDescriptor` method ........................................ 82

**8 An example BeanInfo Object** ................................................ **85**
    Introduction ................................................................... 85
    Objectives ...................................................................... 85
    The `Clock` bean ........................................................... 86
    The `ClockBeanInfo` class ........................................... 88
    The `getIcon()` method ................................................ 90
    The `getPropertyDescriptors()` method ...................... 92
    The `getMethodDescriptors()` method ......................... 93
    Handling bound properties ............................................. 95
    The manifest and JAR files ............................................ 96

**9 Bean Serialization** ............................................................... **99**
    Introduction ................................................................... 99
    Objectives ...................................................................... 99
    Serialization in Java ..................................................... 100
    Serializing a bean ....................................................... 102
    Defining beans that can be serialized .......................... 104

**10 Property Editors and Customizers** ................................. **107**
    Introduction ................................................................. 107
    Objectives .................................................................... 107
    Changing property values ........................................... 108
    The Property Sheet ..................................................... 109
    Property Views ............................................................ 109
    Property Editors .......................................................... 111
    The `PropertyEditor` interface .................................. 111
    The `PropertyEditorSupport` class .......................... 114
    Registering a PropertyEditor ....................................... 116
    Customizers ................................................................. 117

**11 JavaBeans and ActiveX** .................................................. **123**
    Introduction ................................................................. 123
    Objectives .................................................................... 123
    The Component Object Model ..................................... 123
    What is ActiveX? ......................................................... 125
    ActiveX bridge ............................................................. 125
    Packaging a Bean ....................................................... 126
    Creating an ActiveX component ................................... 128
    Using the ActiveX component in a container ................ 132
    Runtime support .......................................................... 134

**12 Event Adapters** ........................................................................................ **135**
    Introduction ............................................................................................ 135
    Objectives ............................................................................................... 135
    Event adapters ....................................................................................... 135
    The use of event adapters ..................................................................... 137
    Defining event adapters ........................................................................ 138

**13 RMI and Beans** ........................................................................................ **141**
    Introduction ............................................................................................ 141
    Objectives ............................................................................................... 141
    Non-graphical beans .............................................................................. 142
    Remote Method Invocation .................................................................... 143
    the `RMIClientBean` .............................................................................. 148
    The Manifest file .................................................................................... 149
    Building the JAR file ............................................................................... 150
    Using the RMI bean ............................................................................... 150

**Appendix A: The `Clock` Bean** .................................................................... **151**

**Appendix B: The `Monitor` Bean** ............................................................... **155**

**Appendix C: The `Alarm` Bean** ................................................................... **159**

**Appendix D: The Multiplexer** ..................................................................... **165**

**Appendix E: RMI beans** .............................................................................. **167**

**Index** ............................................................................................................ **171**

# Content Summary

Chapter 1: Introduction to JavaBeans
This chapter introduces the concept of software component models and JavaBeans in particular. It will also try to answer the following questions:

- Is this book for you?
- How to use this book.
- What you need on your computer to use JavaBeans.
- How to get the JDK.
- How to get the BDK.
- Program conventions.

Chapter 2: Using the BeanBox
This chapter introduces the BeanBox bean builder tool. It will explain how to run it, what it looks like and how to use it. It therefore provides a complete user guide to the BeanBox.

Chapter 3: The Delegation Event Model
The Delegation Event Model was introduced in JDK 1.1 to support both the GUI facilities in Java and JavaBeans. It is introduced in this chapter in order to provide a solid foundation for the remainder of the book.

Chapter 4: Building basic beans
This chapter explains how a very simple bean can be created. It presents two simple beans that can be connected together in the BeanBox. This aims to get the reader going with JavaBeans.

Chapter 5: Property data types
This chapter presents each of the types of property currently supported by JavaBeans (e.g. simple, indexed, constrained). It presents source code illustrating how to define each type.

Chapter 6: Reflection and bean introspection
This chapter introduces the Reflection API in Java and examines how the introspection process works in JavaBeans.

Chapter 7: `BeanInfo` objects
This chapter describes how a `BeanInfo` object is defined. Again source code will illustrate how the `BeanInfo` interface, `SimpleBeanInfo` class and additional `BeanInfo` classes can be defined.

Chapter 8: An example `BeanInfo` object
This chapter presents a worked example of how to define a complete `BeanInfo` object for the `Clock` bean.

Chapter 9: Bean Serialization (persistence)
This chapter introduces the concept of serialization and illustrates how it can be used to serialize a bean.

Chapter 10: Property editors and customizers
In this chapter we describe how customizers are created.

Chapter 11: JavaBeans and ActiveX
This chapter describes the JavaBeans/ActiveX bridge.

Chapter 12: Event adapters
This chapter discusses event adapters: what they are and how they can be used to add an event delivery policy between sources of events and objects which handle those events (listeners).

# 1 Introduction to JavaBeans

## Introduction

This chapter sets the scene for the remainder of this book. It tries to demystify some of the terminology associated with JavaBeans as well as introduce the basic JavaBeans concepts. As such it is a (relatively) non-technical introduction to the subject matter of the rest of the book. You should not be fooled into thinking that JavaBeans is a complex or difficult subject – the majority of the complexity (at least for the basic use of JavaBeans) is primarily due to the terminology used. So don't be put off and don't be intimidated. Just have a go – you might be surprised how far you get and how quickly you get there!

## Objectives

Upon completion of this chapter you will be able to:

- Define JavaBeans.
- Explain the relationship between JavaBeans and other component models.
- Describe a property, method and event.
- Explain what a bean actually is.
- Explain what a bean's published protocol is.
- Obtain the Beans Development Kit (BDK).

# Is this book for you?

This book assumes that you are familiar with the Java programming language, with the definitions of classes, instance variables and methods and that you are comfortable with the creation of objects (or instances) from classes and with calling methods on those objects. It is also assumes that you have some experience of using windows-type programs (such as word processors and drawing packages).

The documentation provided with JavaBeans includes a simple tutorial. This book expands on such material, but does not cover every minute detail. However, it does provide a very fast route into this subject. The many source code examples are backed up by illustrations and helpful guidance.

# How to use this book

You can use this book as a guide to JavaBeans by reading it from start to finish. You can also dip into it to understand various aspects of JavaBeans as and when you need to. It does not attempt to be a complete in-depth guide to every aspect of JavaBeans (for example, it does not cover Enterprise Beans nor does it cover the new mechanisms added in the Glasgow release of JavaBeans to support enterprise-wide computing. Nor does it consider the use of JavaBeans outside the BeanBox or how adapters are implemented. Instead, it focuses on those elements you need to know to get on and use JavaBeans effectively (including linking JavaBeans to ActiveX components).

In general the book takes a very "hands on" approach to the whole subject and assumes that you will implement the examples as you progress.

# Why have software components?

It is generally excepted that software reuse can be a good thing. That is, if you don't need to reinvent the wheel then don't. Thus if you already have some software available which will provide part or all of the functionality you require, then reuse that software rather than try to write it from scratch. Classes in object oriented languages such as Java are one example of how software can be reused. However, they are not the only way in which software can be reused. Another approach is to use a software component.

A software component is a reusable piece of software that can be plugged into other software to provide a specific function. Components differ from classes in that a user of a software component need never examine the source code of a component to use it. Instead, a software component will provide a published interface (or protocol) which states what the user of the component can do.

Therefore the primary difference between classes and components is that a component is a black box, whereas a class can be examined, subclassed and modified (in a subclass). As such, components are simpler to use.

It is also useful to note that very many man-made systems are constructed from components. For example, in a computer various different components are plugged together via predefined interfaces. Thus the construction of software from components is actually very natural.

# What are JavaBeans?

JavaBeans is an architecture for the definition and reuse of software components. The Beans Development Kit 1.0 (BDK) was first released in February 1997. The BDK contains the JavaBeans API sources, (the class files are already part of the JDK 1.1), the BeanBox test container and some examples, as well as tutorial documentation.

What is the JavaBeans architecture for? The primary aim is to allow developers and third-party software vendors to supply reusable components in a simple to use and unified manner. For example, you might wish to incorporate a simple word processor into your application. This word processor might be available as a "Bean". It would then be possible to add this bean to your application without the need to refine the bean. Sun intend that most beans should be reusable software components that can be manipulated visually in some sort of builder tool. Thus, in the case of the word processor bean we might select it from a menu and drop it onto an application, positioning its visual representation (i.e. the text writing area) as required. Of course, the facilities provided by a builder tool will depend both on the types of component being used as well as the intended use of the builder. Examples of such builders, cited in the JavaBeans 1.0 API Specification, include visual application builders, GUI layout builders, Web page builders or even server application builders. Indeed, sometimes the "builder tool" may simply be an editor (such as a word processor) that includes some beans as part of a larger document. Beans can also be used directly by programmers (as indeed anyone who uses any of the components in the AWT is already doing).

JavaBeans may vary in size and complexity. Simple ones may be buttons or sliders; other more complex examples may be database viewers, word processors or spreadsheets. Although in practice, it is expected that bean components will be small to medium-sized controls.

# JavaBeans and other component models

The Beans component model is intended to be similar in concept to Visual Basic's VBX and OCX component architecture and to Delphi's VCL, but without the need to follow a rigid programming model. This makes the generation of Beans simpler, but at times requires the developer to define numerous methods for accessing Bean properties.

Beans differ from class libraries in that they are intended for visual manipulation and customisation via their properties, while class libraries are intended for programmatic use and for customisation either, through instantiation or via subclassing[1]. Thus the new JDBC API is not a bean, although a database access bean for Sybase would make sense. Such a bean would be built on top of the JDBC.

It is intended that JavaBeans should be architecture neutral, except where they interface to the underlying platform. Thus beans which handle buttons will be independent of the platform on which they will be run. In contrast, a bridge between JavaBeans and Microsoft's ActiveX has already been released (March 1997) and allows a bean to use the ActiveX facilities. Other bridges are being actively developed to Live Connect (for Netscape Navigator) and Live Object (née OpenDoc). The intention is that a given bean will use the appropriate platform features but will present a common face to the Java environment. This has actually been one of the largest constraints on the development of JavaBeans and it has taken a lot of work to ensure that the various bean APIs can be cleanly converted to these component models.

---

[1] Having said this, it is still possible to use beans programmatically.

# The JavaBeans package

One of the most confusing elements in JavaBeans is the use of the `java.beans` package and the BDK. The `java.beans` package provides classes and interfaces which are primarily useful to programmers who are developing tools to support and manipulate Beans. The BDK provides additional support for the JavaBeans API, a test Bean development tool (the "BeanBox") sample Beans and documentation. In the example presented here, you will notice that no classes or interfaces provided by either are used. The only element used is the BeanBox tool. This is because any class can be treated as a Bean as long as certain naming conventions are followed, although any Bean which will have a visual representation must be a descendant of `java.awt.Component`.

# Bean terminology

A JavaBean is defined via its interface. That is, the interface presented by the bean to its user indicates what it can be made to do. There are three things that comprise this interface: its properties, its events and its methods. These are discussed briefly below:

**Properties** These are the attributes of the Bean that can be modified by anything outside the Bean. They are often referred to as being *published* or *exposed* by the Bean. In effect, a property is an instance variable which is accessed via specific `get` and `set` methods. For example, if we have a property `max`, then we would have:

- an instance variable `max`,
- `setMax(-)` and `getMax( )` methods.

Note that the methods which are used to set and get the value of the property max have the format `set<property name>` and `get<property name>`, with the name of the variable starting with an upper-case letter. This will be discussed again in more detail later.

**Events** These are used to allow one component to communicate with another component. The event model used is the Delegation Event

Model introduced to the AWT (Abstract Window Toolkit) in JDK 1.1.

**Methods** These are public methods (which do not match the naming conventions used in Beans) that can be used to directly request some service of a Bean.

# Builder Tool support

JavaBeans are intended to be used with builder tools that allow a user to construct an application or applet interactively. These tools rely on being able to interrogate a bean to find out what it can do and what it offers. Using this information a builder tool can provide interactive and graphical ways of connecting beans together. The Beans Development Kit provides a very simple builder tool called the BeanBox. This tool is far from being a fully fledged builder tool; however, it does allow you to test your beans, provides a minimum level of functionality and is free!

# Building an application

In order to give you an idea of how you might use JavaBeans, consider the following example. Let us assume that we wish to create an egg-timer application. We already have the following beans:

- a clock bean which issues a "tick" at regular intervals (for example every second),
- a monitor bean which counts the number of times it is triggered by another bean. When a predefined number of triggers are received it generates an event,
- an alarm bean which when triggered generates an alarm.

These beans can be connected together so that the clock bean sends a "tick" to the monitor bean each second (see Figure 1.1). Once the monitor bean reaches a maximum number of ticks (say 60) it then sends an event to the alarm bean telling it to raise an alarm.

The result is that we have produced an egg-timer application merely by connecting these three beans together (indeed, if we had used a builder tool it would have been done without writing any code at all!). Notice that these beans may not have been written to be connected together in this way. For example, a clock bean that generates ticks at regular intervals is useful in very many applications.

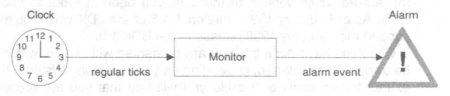

Figure 1.1: The egg-timer application

# What you need to use JavaBeans

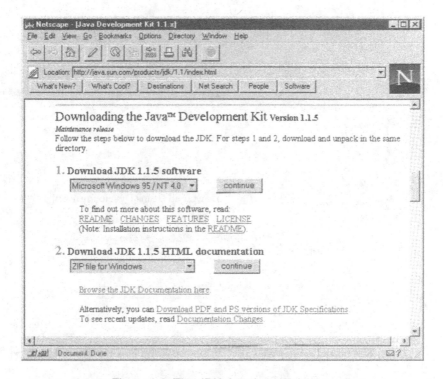

Figure 1.2: The JDK download Web page

To use JavaBeans and the Beans Development Kit (BDK) you first need to have the Java Development Kit (JDK) installed on your computer. You can obtain this by downloading the appropriate JDK for your platform from `http://java.sun.com/`. Figure 1.2 illustrates the download Web page provided by Sun. Note you need to make sure which version of the JDK you need in order to use the BDK. As of February 1998, version 1.1.5 of the JDK was required to support the February 1998 release of the BDK 1.0.

Once you have done this you are presented within a file which can be unzipped (or untarred, depending on your operating system). If you extract the contents of this file you will find that you are presented within a program which can install the JDK for you. This is relatively straightforward. Note, however, that the documentation must be downloaded separately (again in a zipped or tarred file).

## How to get the BDK

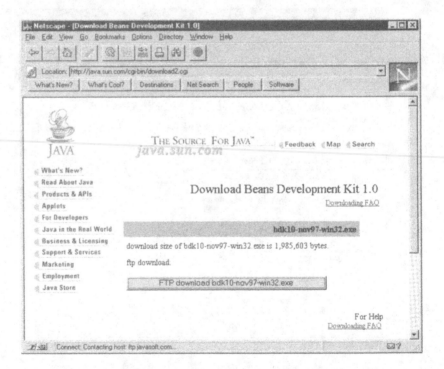

Figure 1.3: The BDK download web page

You can obtain the Beans Development Kit (BDK) via a Web page relating to the JavaBeans project. This is maintained by Sun at `http://java.sun.com/beans/`. The Web page used to download the BDK is illustrated in Figure 1.3. As you can see from this figure, the download process is very straightforward. Essentially, the FTP protocol is used to copy the install program to you computer.

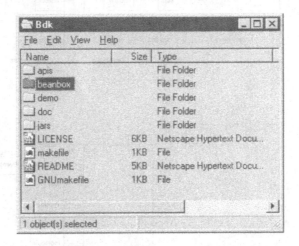

Figure 1.4: The BDK top-level directories

To download the BDK release for Windows/x86, select "Microsoft Windows" from the "Select Installer" pop-up menu below and then click on the "Download Software" button (for a Unix system select "Unix"). Next use your browser to save the .exe file into a local disk file (on a Unix system save the .sh file). After downloading, you can install the release by double clicking on the .exe file. This will bring up a standard Windows InstallShield installer (on a Unix platform you can unpack the release anywhere you like using the sh file). For Win32 platforms Sun also provide an additional installer that will automatically install the installer for the JavaBeans Bridge for ActiveX 1.0. Double-click on the Bridge installer if you want to install the ActiveX Bridge. An introduction to the release is available in \bdk\README.html.

The final result will be that a set of subdirectories are created on your computers hard disk containing the BeanBox, demonstration programs, documentation and a set of jar files (more about these later). The BDK top-level directories are illustrated in Figure 1.4 while the whole directory structure is illustrated in Figure 1.5.

## What you get in the BDK

The BDK (as of February 1998) contains:

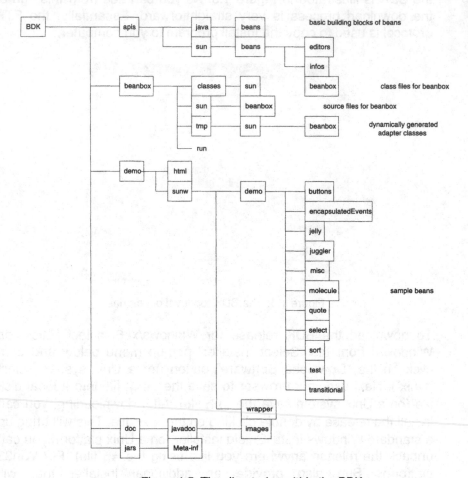

Figure 1.5: The directories within the BDK

- The JavaBeans API sources. These are provided as `.java` reference sources in the `apis` subdirectory.
- The BeanBox builder tool. This allows you to test out your new Beans against a reference container, and also acts an example of how to build a Bean container.
- Fifteen example Beans are provided which can run in the BeanBox and demonstrate various Bean behaviours.
- A variety of reference source code.
- Makefile information.
- A tutorial in PostScript and Adobe Acrobat (PDF) explaining the main JavaBeans 1.0 concepts using the BeanBox.

# Program conventions

In the remainder of this book `courier` is used to identify source code. For example:

```
a = 2 + 3;
```

All reserved words are in bold (e.g. **class**, **for**, **if**) and all menu options, such as **Load** from the **File** menu, are in bold.

# 2 Using the BeanBox

## Introduction

The BeanBox tool is provided as part of the BDK. It is a simple builder tool which provides all the basic elements of much more powerful (but expensive) builder tools. It allows bean developers to construct simple applets as well as test their own beans. It is provided with a default set of beans. This allows you to start working with beans before you attempt to implement your own (the source code for these is available in the demo subdirectory of the BDK).

## Objectives

Once you have completed this chapter you will be able to:

- Use the BeanBox to test beans.
- Change the properties of a bean using the PropertySheet window.
- Link beans together in various ways.
- Save and restore your applications.

13

## Starting the BeanBox

The start the BeanBox tool you need to be in the BDK directory. In this directory you will find a subdirectory called BeanBox. This directory contains a file called run.bat (use run.sh for Unix platforms). To start running the BeanBox you merely need to type in run (run.sh on a Unix platform). This is illustrated in Figure 2.1. The result of starting the BeanBox is illustrated in Figure 2.2. Note if you experience problems when attempting to run the BeanBox, check to see whether the Java Development Kit 1.1 (JDK 1.1) is in your path. If not, then the Java virtual machine (JVM) will not be found and the BeanBox will not be able to execute.

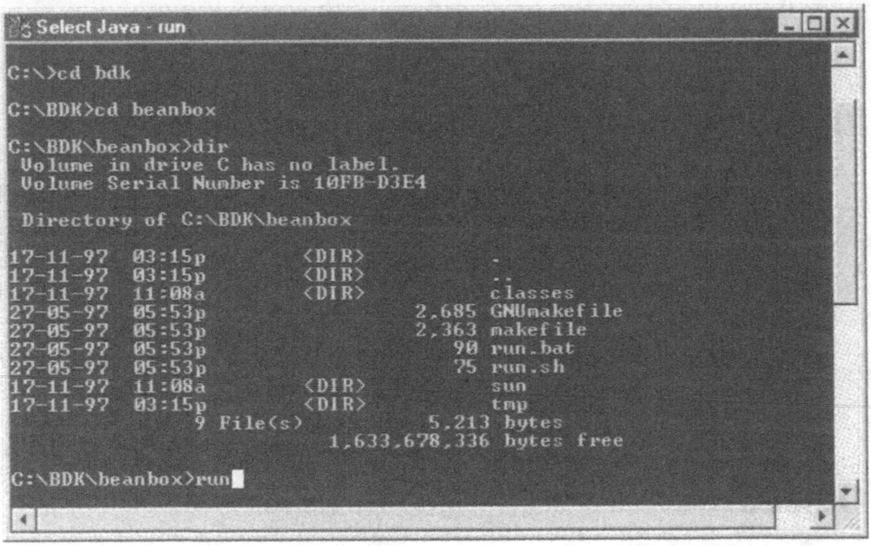

Figure 2.1: Starting the BeanBox tool

## The BeanBox

The result of running the BeanBox are the three windows illustrated in Figure 2.2. As you can see from this figure, the three windows are labelled "ToolBox", "BeanBox" and "PropertySheet". The ToolBox window provides a palette for the beans currently available. The BeanBox window provides a drawing (or composition) area within which you can construct your applications from the available beans. The PropertySheet window allows you to modify the properties of the currently selected Bean. For the moment, just accept that a property of a bean is something like the colour of a bean, or the label it displays etc. In the figure the PropertySheet is displaying the properties of the BeanBox window itself (this actually gives away that the BeanBox is constructed from beans!).

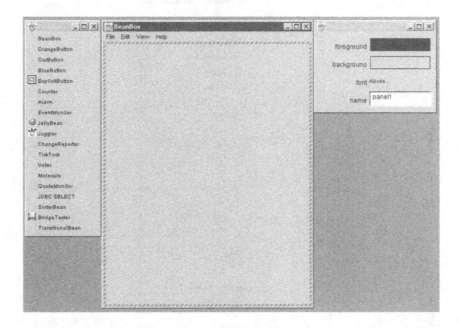

Figure 2.2: The BeanBox windows

## The ToolBox palette

The ToolBox palette (illustrated in greater detail in Figure 2.3) changes depending upon which beans are currently loaded into the BeanBox. By default, when the BeanBox starts up it loads all the beans it can find in a subdirectory calls `jars` of the BDK directory. If you look in this directory you will find that the files there all have a `.jar` extension. This is because they are Java Archive (or JAR) files. These jar files contain the Beans. Later in this book, when you come to create your own beans, you will put them in jar files in order that the BeanBox can read them.

To select a bean to use in the BeanBox window, you first click on the bean you want (note that there is no visual confirmation of the selected bean) and then click in the BeanBox window. The select bean will then appear. Have a go – don't worry about selecting the wrong beans; you can't. We are just trying to put any bean into the BeanBox. Once you have done this, select the **Clear** menu option from the **File** menu of the BeanBox.

Figure 2.3: The ToolBox palette

## The BeanBox window

The BeanBox window itself is resizable, so you do not need to work with the default size window, which is actually quite large. In Figure 2.4 it has been resized to a more manageable size. Notice that there is a hashed boundary around the window. This indicates the currently selected bean, in this case the BeanBox itself. When you add new beans to the BeanBox you will notice that the hashed boundary is removed from the BeanBox and appears around the new bean instead. Thus indicating that the new bean is the currently selected bean. You should also notice that the details in the PropertySheet window change.

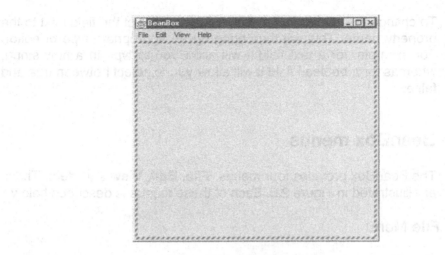

Figure 2.4: The BeanBox window

# The PropertySheet window

The details displayed by the PropertySheet window change depending upon which bean is currently selected. For example, Figure 2.4 illustrates the PropertySheet window for the BeanBox. This PropertySheet illustrates that a BeanBox can have a foreground and background colour, a selected font and a name. By contrast, the PropertySheet in Figure 2.9 illustrates the details for an ExplicitButton bean (one of the beans listed in the ToolBox palette in Figure 2.3).

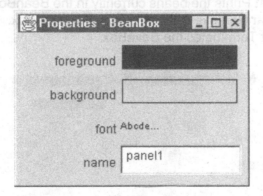

Figure 2.4: The BeanBox properties

To change the value of a property you must select the field next to the property name. This will then bring up an appropriate type of editor. For example, for a text field it will allow you to type in a new string, whereas for a boolean field it will allow you to select between true and false.

# The BeanBox menus

The BeanBox provides four menus: **File**, **Edit**, **View** and **Help**. These are illustrated in Figure 2.5. Each of these menus is described below.

## The **File** Menu

The **File** menu provides options for saving your work, clearing all beans from the BeanBox, loading more beans and printing the beans in the BeanBox. Each **File** menu option is briefly described below:

- **Save** Allows you to save the state of your work so that you can continue working with your application at a later stage.
- **SerializeComponent** Save the state of an individual bean (we will look at this again later in the book).
- **MakeApplet** Create an applet from your bean-based application.
- **Load** Allows you to load a previously saved set of beans.
- **LoadJar** Load additional JAR files containing beans. These beans will be added to the ToolBox palette. Note that if you load a JAR file containing beans already in the ToolBox palette they will be duplicated on the palette!
- **Print** Prints the beans currently in the BeanBox to a printer.
- **Clear** Removes all beans from the BeanBox.
- **Exit** Terminates the BeanBox.

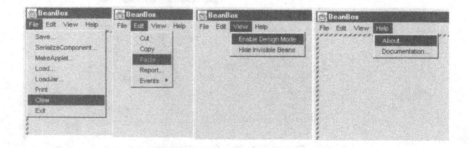

Figure 2.5: The BeanBox menus

# The **Edit** Menu

The **Edit** menu provides the standard **Cut**, **Copy** and **Paste** options. These are used to delete, copy and paste beans within the BeanBox. In addition, the **Edit** menu includes a **Report** option. This can be used to obtain information about the currently selected bean. We will look at this again later in the book. The remaining **Edit** menu options will differ depending on the currently selected bean. For example, in Figure 2.5 the **Edit** menu includes an option **Events**. This can be used to link the triggering of an event with a method on another bean. We will look at this in more detail later in this chapter.

# The **View** Menu

The **View** menu has two options: **Disable Design Mode** and **Hide Invisible Beans** (illustrated in Figure 2.6). We shall look at the first of these options in more detail below.

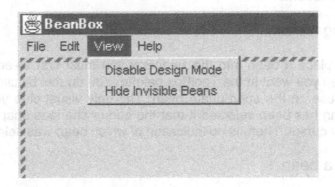

Figure 2.6: The **View** menu

**Disable Design Mode** When you initiate the BeanBox you are automatically put into design mode. This allows you to place beans into the BeanBox, connect them together and edit them. This means that in addition to the BeanBox window you have access to the ToolBox palette and the PropertySheet. However, you can turn off the design mode. In this mode, the ToolBox palette and the PropertySheet widows are hidden. You can no longer edit beans or change the way they interact. In effect, you are presented with a running application. Indeed, when you turn off design mode you are essentially in *run-time mode*. This is one way in which you can present an application you have constructed using the BeanBox to a user.

## The **Help** Menu

The **Help** menu has two options: **About** and **Documentation**. The **About** option gives you information on the version of the BeanBox that you are using, while **Documentation** currently tells you to use a browser to view a specified HTML file. This may change in future releases of the BDK.

# Working with beans

Now that you have started the BeanBox and are familiar with each of the menus, you are ready to start to work with some beans. We shall use the `ExplicitButton` bean as the guinea pig for our experiments.

## Selecting a bean

To place a bean into the BeanBox you must first select the type of bean you want in the ToolBox palette. You do this by clicking with the mouse on the appropriate bean. The only visual clue you get that a bean has been selected it that the cursor changes shape to a cross-hair cursor. There is no indication of which bean was selected.

## Placing a bean

Next you must click in the BeanBox. The selected bean is now displayed in the BeanBox centred on the position of the mouse when you clicked the mouse button. The result of doing this for the `ExplicitButton` bean is illustrated in Figure 2.7.

Note that the hashed boundary is now around the `ExplicitButton` illustrating that it is the currently selected bean. You are now in a position to modify its properties.

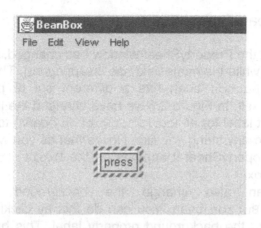

Figure 2.7: Placing a bean in the BeanBox

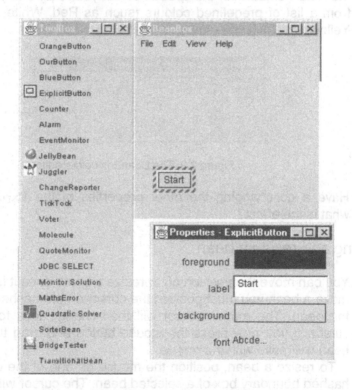

Figure 2.8: Changing the properties of an `ExplicitButton` bean

## Changing a beans properties

Notice that the PropertySheet window has changed. It now includes a label field (while the name field has disappeared). This is because the `ExplicitButton` bean has a different set of properties to the BeanBox itself. In Figure 2.9 we have changed the label from "press" (the default label for all `ExplicitButton` beans) to "Start". You can change it to any string you like. Notice that as you type the new label into the PropertySheet it appears on the `ExplicitButton` bean in the BeanBox.

You can also change the background colour of the `ExplicitButton` bean. You can do this by clicking on the colour field next to the background property label. This brings up a (very) simple colour editor, as illustrated in Figure 2.9. You can either type in the RGB numbers for the specific colour you require or you can select from a list of predefined colours (such as Red, White, Green, Blue, Yellow).

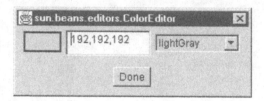

Figure 2.9: The BeanBox colour editor

Have a go changing the other properties of the `ExplicitBean` - what is the effect?

## Moving and resize a bean

You can move the position of, or resize a bean, once it is selected. To move a bean you must position the cursor on the hashed boundary of the bean. The mouse cursor will then change to a four-way arrow cursor. If you now press the mouse button and drag the mouse the bean will move with the mouse.

To resize a bean, position the mouse on one of the corners of the hashed boundary box of a selected bean. The cursor will then change shape to a diagonal arrow pointing into a right angle. If you now press the mouse button and drag the mouse, the bean will change size (as appropriate for the type of bean involved).

# Customizers

Some beans also provide a customizer. A customizer is similar in concept to a wizard. It allows a user to change specific details of a bean without necessarily being aware of all the properties involved.

If a bean provides a customizer, then a **Customize** entry is added to the **Edit** menu. For example, if you place a JDBC Select bean in the BeanBox and select its customizer then a new dialog window is opened.

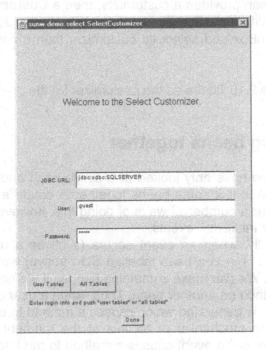

Figure 2.10: The JDBC Select customizer

# Moving and resize a bean

You can move the position of, or resize a bean, once it is selected. To move a bean you must position the cursor on the hashed boundary of the bean. The mouse cursor will then change to a four-way arrow cursor. If you now press the mouse button and drag the mouse the bean will move with the mouse.

To resize a bean, position the mouse on one of the corners of the hashed boundary box of a selected bean. The cursor will then change shape to a diagonal arrow pointing into a right angle. If you now press the mouse button and drag the mouse, the bean will change size (as appropriate for the type of bean involved).

## Customizers

Some beans also provide a customizer. A customizer is similar in concept to a wizard. It allows a user to change specific details of a bean without necessarily being aware of all the properties involved.

If a bean provides a customizer, then a **Customize** entry is **added** to the Edit menu. For example, if `you place` a JDBC Select bean in the BeanBox and select its customizer then a new dialog window is opened.

Figure 2.10 illustrates the customizer for the `JDBC Select` bean.

# Connecting beans together

So far we have only looked at a single bean and its properties. It is now time to link some beans together to create a simple application. There are a number of ways of doing this; however, we will start with the most intuitive – events.

Essentially, when an event occurs (such as a user clicking on the `ExplicitButton` bean labelled Start above) we want something to happen. We can make something happen if we have linked this event to a method on another bean. Thus, when a user clicks on the button, an event is generated which causes a method to execute (don't worry about the mechanics of all this at the moment. We will look into exactly how the event causes a method to run later – for the moment just accept that it does).

Figure 2.11: The Juggler bean

To illustrate this we need to add another bean to the BeanBox. We are going to use the example presented in many JavaBeans tutorials, as it is easily understood and available in the BeanBox. This example will make use of the Duke animation bean (labelled Juggler in the ToolBox palette). You should therefore add the `Juggler` bean to the BeanBox. You should also add a second `ExplicitButton` bean to the BeanBox, such that you end up with a BeanBox similar to that illustrated in Figure 2.11.

You now have a BeanBox containing three beans. However, these beans do not actually do anything yet. You need to connect them together, as outlined above.

The first thing we will do is to link the Start button to the `Juggler` bean. This is done by first selecting the Start button (so that the hashed border is displayed around it). Next go to the **Edit** menu and select the **Events** option. This will bring up a submenu with two options on it (see Figure 2.12). Select the **button push** option (as we want to handle events generated when the button is clicked). This brings up a menu with a single option: **actionPerformed**. If you think back to the Java AWT and the `Button` class, you will know that this is the method which an `ActionListener` must implement in order to handle events generated by buttons. In other words, it is the method which is run in response to an ActionEvent being raised. It would therefore be in this method that you would define what should happen when a button is clicked. This is exactly what this set of menus represents.

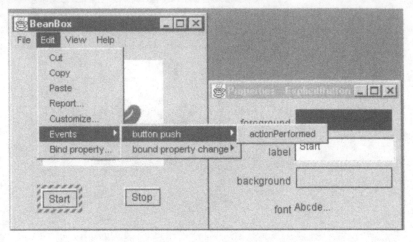

Figure 2.12: Selecting the **actionPerformed** menu option

Having selected the **actionPerformed** menu option you will find that a red "rubberband" line now appears. This line is rooted on the Start button, but follows the cursor as you move the mouse. This line indicates that you must link the Start button with a target bean. That is a bean that will perform some operation.

You should now move the cursor over the Juggler (which will be the target bean) and click the mouse button. This will start the process of linking the two beans together. This is illustrated in Figure 2:13.

When you select the Juggler bean a new window will appear which lists all the public methods available on the Juggler bean. This window is called the EventTargetDialog window. The methods displayed by this window can be called in response to an event being generated. We shall select the startJuggling method. This is illustrated in Figure 2.14. This therefore means that when a user clicks on the Start button, the startJuggling method of the Juggler bean will be executed. This method starts Duke juggling.

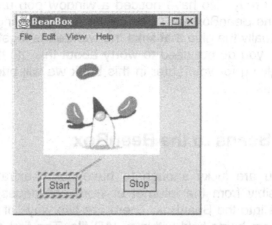

Figure 2.13: Linking the Start button and the Juggler

You should now follow the same steps for the second button (which you might like to re-label Stop), except that you should link it to the `stopJuggling` method.

If you do this, you will have a simple application containing two buttons and an animation, which will allow a user to start and stop Duke juggling. Have a go and try it out. Notice how simple it was to create this application.

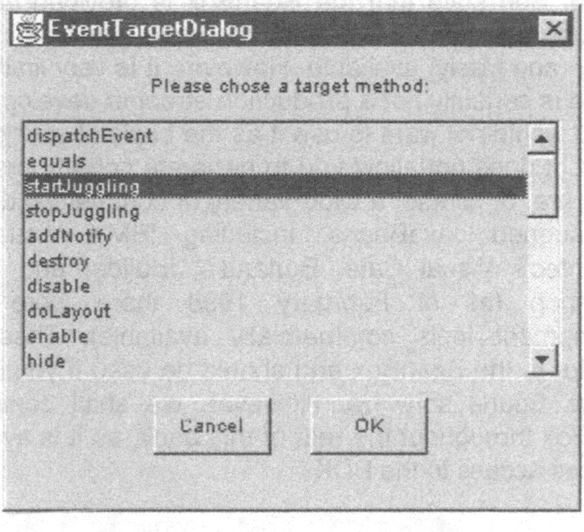

Figure 2.14: The EventTargetDialog window

You may also have noticed a window pop up which informed you that the BeanBox was "Generating and compiling adapter class". This is actually the glue that links the two beans together. However, at this stage you do not need to worry about this, as the BeanBox does all the gluing for you. Later in this book we will briefly look into adapter classes.

## Adding Beans to the BeanBox

If you are lucky enough to have some extra beans to play with (possibly from the Internet or from colleagues) then you can load these into the BeanBox. There are two ways of doing this - both rely on them being held within a JAR file. The first and easiest way is to place the jar file in the `jar` directory of the BDK. The beans will then be automatically loaded into the BeanBox when it is next started up. Alternatively, you can use the **LoadJar** option from the **File** menu. We shall look in more detail at JAR files in Chapter 4.

## Builder tools

The BeanBox is only intended as an experimental environment. Indeed, Sun state that the BeanBox is provided as a tool to allow developers to test their beans. We have used it in this book, as it is widely (and freely) available. However, it is very limited in what it can do and is certainly not a production strength development editor. That is, you would not want to use it as the basis of your development. For a start, it does not allow you to generate code to create applications. There are, of course, a wide variety of commercial development tools that support JavaBeans, including IBM's VisualAge for Java, Symantec's Visual Café, Borland's JBuilder and Sun's own Java Workshop (as of February 1998 there were 29 JavaBeans development tools commercially available). These tools are far superior to the BeanBox and should be used if you intend to develop serious Beans software. However, we shall continue to use the BeanBox throughout the rest of this book, as it is available to anyone who has access to the BDK.

# 3 *The Delegation*
# *Event Model*

## Introduction

In release 1.1 of the Java Development Kit (JDK 1.1) a new event-handling model was introduced. This model was called the Delegation Event Model. Although it is extensively used in the Abstract Window Toolkit (AWT) of the JDK, it was originally designed for the JavaBeans architecture. It is the mechanism by which one bean informs another bean that something has happened or that it wants that bean to perform some action. It is therefore very important to understand how the Delegation Event Model works. This chapter provides an introduction to this event-handling model – if you are already familiar with it you may wish to move on to the next chapter.

## Objectives

Once you have finished this chapter you will be able to:

- Create an event and implement a listener to handle the event.
- Create new events from existing event classes.
- Define new listener interfaces for new categories of events.
- Understand the difference between multicast and unicast sources.

- Explain the Delegation Event Model used through Java 1.1 (and later).

# Background

The event model in the original version of Java relied on a component handling an event itself. If it did not handle the event (or if it wished to allow another object to receive the event as well), the event was passed to the object containing the original receiver of the event. This was referred to as the Event Containment Hierarchy. The problem with this approach was that not only was it difficult to work with (as the way in which components were structured in terms of containers determined the order in which objects processed the event), but it was inefficient. For example, a window might have two containers, each of which contained a number of containers within which graphic components (such as buttons) were displayed. If the developer wanted to group all the event-handling behaviour in the top level window, then each event would be passed from the graphic component to the first container and then to the next container before reaching the window.

For JavaBeans, which relies heavily on events for its basic infrastructure, this was not acceptable. What was required was a more efficient, lighter weight approach. The Delegation Event Model was the result. For those of you familiar with the Containment Event Model, it may at first appear that the Delegation Event Model is more complex. In some ways it is, as it is also more flexible and more powerful. However, once you have got used to this event model it is a very natural way to build systems.

# What is an event?

What is an event? This question has two answers, depending on whether you are referring to the concept or to events in Java. We shall consider each answer.

An event is an asynchronous piece of data that is generated in response to some condition being met or some action being performed. For example, in a windowing system an event might be raised when a mouse button is clicked,or when a key is pressed etc. If the cursor was over a button when the mouse button was pressed then an event might be raised for the button (an `ActionEvent`).

However, user interfaces are not the only things that might result in an event being raised. For example, a timer might be set to raise an event when a set period of time has elapsed. This event may then be sent to an object that needs to know that this elapsed time has been reached, etc.

In terms of the Java language an event is an object which describes what actually happened. It is thus an instance of a class. There are a number of different event classes in Java, some of which are illustrated in Figure 3.1.

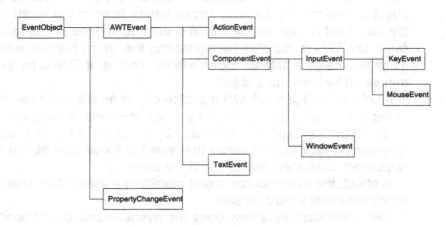

Figure 3.1: Event classes in Java

When you need to create an event you must therefore instantiate one of these classes. In turn, when you receive an event, what you actually receive is an instance of one of these classes.

As all events are instances of Event classes you can examine the JavaDoc documentation relating to each class. From this you can find that all events will respond to the getSource() and toString() methods. The first of these returns the object within which the event was generated and the second returns a string representation of the event.

# Delegating responsibility for an event

We have already said that JavaBeans uses the Delegation Event Model and that this model is better than the original event-handling model, but what does this event model do?

Essentially it does just what the name says: it delegates responsibility for handling an event to one object that may not be the object that acted as the source of the event. This is illustrated in Figure 3.2.

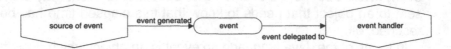

Figure 3.2: Delegating an event

That is relatively straightforward. The next thing we need to think about is how an event source knows where to send the event it has created. That is, how do we tell an event source who to delegate the event to? This is handled by registering the event handler with the event source as a listener for its events. That is, it *listens* for events generated by the source object.

An object is registered with a source object as a listener using one of the add<type of event>listener methods (for example, the addActionListener() method). Thus when an event source generates a new event it sends that event to those objects that have registered as listeners (handlers) of the event.

In effect, the event source object maintains a list of other objects to which the event should be sent.

The next question is how does the event source object send the event to the listener objects? In actual fact, this is very straightforward and relies on nothing more complex than a procedure call. That is, the new event is passed to the listener objects by calling the appropriate listener object method with the event as a parameter. For example, a button object will pass an action event to a button event listener by calling the actionPerformed() method on the button event listener. This is illustrated in Figure 3.3 (note that the object handling the event raised by the button object is called the button handler in this figure).

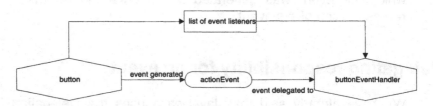

Figure 3.3: A button event handler

Notice that the `button` maintains a list of event handlers. This indicates that more than one object may be sent the event. This is known as multicasting events.

You may well be wondering how the event source knows which method to call. This is determined by the Listener interface implemented by the handler object. For example, the `buttonEventHandler` would have implemented the `ActionListener` interface. This interface requires that the `actionPerformed(ActionEvent)` method is implemented. As the method used to register listener objects (handlers) with the button requires an object whose class implemented the `ActionListener` interface, the button can be sure that all its listeners will respond to the `actionPerformed(ActionEvent)` method.

Different objects require different interfaces to be implemented by their handler objects. Table 3.1 lists the interfaces defined for the AWT, the methods they define and the objects that fire the events handled by the classes which implement the listeners.

Table 3.1: The listeners used with the Delegation Event Model in the AWT

| Interface | Triggered methods | Originating object |
|---|---|---|
| ActionListener | actionPerformed (ActionEvent) | Button, List, MenuItem, TextField |
| ItemListener | itemStateChanged (ItemEvent) | Checkbox, Choice CheckboxMenuItem, |
| WindowListener The argument to these methods is WindowEvent | windowClosing windowOpened windowIconified windowDeiconified windowClosed windowActivated windowDeactivated | Dialog, Frame |
| ComponentListener The argument to these methods is ComponentEvent | componentMoved componentHidden componentResized componentShown | Dialog, Frame |
| AdjustmentListener | adjustmentValueChanged (AdjustmentEvent) | Scrollbar |
| ItemListener | itemStateChanged (ItemEvent) | Checkbox, CheckboxMenuItem, Choice, List |
| MouseMotionListener | mouseDragged(MouseEvent) | Canvas, Dialog, |

| | mouseMoved(MouseEvent) | Frame, Panel, Window |
|---|---|---|
| MouseListener | mousePressed(MouseEvent) | Canvas, Dialog, |
| | mouseReleased(MouseEvent) | Frame, Panel, Window |
| | mouseEntered(MouseEvent) | |
| | mouseExited(MouseEvent) | |
| | mouseClicked(MouseEvent) | |
| KeyListener | keyPressed(KeyEvent) | Component |
| | keyReleased(KeyEvent) | |
| | keyTyped(KeyEvent) | |
| TextListener | textValueChanged(TextEvent) | TextComponent |

# Event Listeners

The Java delegation event model introduced the concept of listeners. Listeners are effectively objects which "listen" for a particular event to occur. When it does they react to it. For example, the event associated with the button might be that it has been "pressed". The listener would then be notified that the button had been pressed and would decide what action to take. This approach involves delegation because the responsibility for handling an event, generated by one object, may be another object's. In general I tend to call a class which implements such a listener interface either a handler or a controller (depending upon exactly what that class is doing). This helps me to separate out the interface specification from the implementation.

# Working with Events

The delegation model changes the way in which users create GUIs. Using this model they define the graphic objects to be displayed, add them to the display and associate them with a listener object. The listener object then handles the events that are generated for that object.

For example, if we wish to create a button which will be displayed on an interface and allow the user to exit without using the border frame buttons, then we need to create a button and a handler for the action on the button. For example,

```
exitButtonHandler = new ExitButtonHandler ();
exitButton = new Button(" Exit ");
exitButton.addActionListener(exitButtonHandler);
```

This code creates a new user-defined listener object, ExitButtonHandler, and then creates a new Button (with a label "Exit"). It then registers the exitButtonHandler as the action listener for the button. That is, it is the object that will *listen* for action events (such as the button being pressed). The ExitButtonHandler class (presented in Listing 3.1) provides a single instance method actionPerformed(ActionEvent) which will initiate the System.exit(0) method.

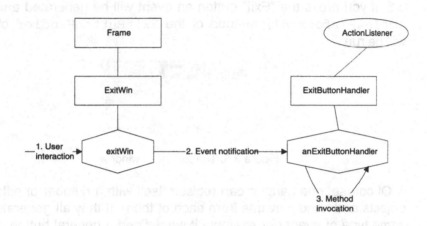

Figure 3.4: The class and object diagram using the Delegation Event Model

The resulting class and instance structures for the complete program presented in Listing 3.1 are illustrated in Figure 3.4. As you can see from this diagram, the separation of interface and control is conceptually very clean.

Listing 3.1: ExitWin

```
import java.awt.*;
import java.awt.event.*;

public class ExitWin extends Frame {
    public static void main(String args []) {
        new ExitWin();
    }
    // ExitWin constructor
    public ExitWin () {
        super("Exit Button Demo");
        ExitButtonHandler handler = new ExitButtonHandler();
        Button exitButton = new Button(" Exit ");
        exitButton.addActionListener(handler);
        add("Center", exitButton);
        pack();
```

```
        setVisible(true);
    }
}
// Handler for exit button
class ExitButtonHandler implements ActionListener {
    public void actionPerformed(ActionEvent event) {
        System.exit(0);
    }
}
```

The result of executing this program is the window displayed in Figure 3.5. If you press the "Exit" button an event will be generated and the `actionPerformed()` method of the `ExitButtonHandler` object will be run.

Figure 3.5: The `ExitWin` window

Of course, one handler can register itself with a number of different objects and handle events from each of them. If they all generate the same type of event (for example if we defined a general button event handler for three buttons) then we would need to identify which event we are dealing with. In the case of buttons there are two ways of doing this: either identify the originating object using `getSource()` or obtain the action command associated with the event. For example:

```
String cmd = event.getActionCommand();
if (cmd.equals("Exit"))
    System.exit(0);
else (cmd.equals("Save"))
    savedata();
else (cmd.equals("New"))
    newdata();
```

The action command associated with an action event from a button is either a string set using the `setActionCommand()` method or the label of the button (if no action command has been explicitly provided).

# Creating new Events

You are not limited to using only the event classes already available. You can define your own event classes to be used with your own listener interfaces. This is particularly useful in JavaBeans and will be used in the next chapter.

As all events are defined by classes, to create your own event you merely subclass the appropriate existing class. For example, in JavaBeans you would normally subclass the `java.util.EventObject` class.

Listing 3.2 illustrates a simple example used to create an event for the monitor bean described in Chapter 1. This bean raises an event when a certain number of tick events have been received. The event generated contains an integer indicating the number of tick events received before the monitor event was triggered.

**Listing 3.2: The `MonitorEvent`**

```
import java.util.EventObject;

public class MonitorEvent extends EventObject {
    int triggerValue = 0;
    public MonitorEvent(Object o) {
        super(o);
    }
    public void setTrigger(int i) {
        triggerValue = i;
    }
    public int getTrigger() {
        return triggerValue;
    }
}
```

Notice that the `MonitorEvent` only defines two accessor methods `setTrigger(int)` and `getTrigger()` which are used to set the `triggerValue` (representing the number of ticks before the event was generated). The remainder of the functionality for the `MonitorEvent` relies on inherited features from `EventObject`. This includes recording the originating object and making that available via `getSource()`.

# Defining new listener interfaces

In order that your beans can use the events you define you will need to provide `add<event type>Listener()` and `remove<event`

`.type>Listener()` methods. These methods will take objects which implement a listener interface as their parameters. You will therefore need to provide listener interfaces for your new event types. In fact, this is actually very useful anyway, as it allows other developers to see what they need to implement in order to work with your beans.

As an example, we shall define a `MonitorEventListener` interface. This interface will define a single (abstract) method called `monitorEventPerformed(MonitorEvent)`. It does not need to implement any other methods, nor does it need to inherit from any class or interface. Listing 3.3 presents this interface.

### Listing 3.3: The `MonitorEventInterface`

```
public interface MonitorEventInterface {
    public void monitorEventPerformed(MonitorEvent event);
}
```

You can now define classes that will implement this interface. For example, the `Alarm` bean (again from Chapter 1) would implement this interface so that it can handle events raised by the `Monitor` bean. For example:

### Listing 3.4: Implementing the `MonitorEventInterface`

```
public class Alarm extends Canvas
                        implements MonitorEventListener {
    public Alarm() {
        ...
    }
    public void monitorEventPerformed(MonitorEvent event){
        triggerArlam();
    }
}
```

The only thing we have left to do with regard to listeners is to look at how we can let the `Monitor` class register classes such as the `Alarm` class as handlers of the `MonitorEvent`.

As was mentioned earlier, registering an object as a handler of an event relies on the `add<event type>Listener()` and `remove<event type>Listener()` methods. These registration methods are relatively straightforward. They rely on the object being passed to them implementing a specific interface. These objects are then recorded in a list (typically a `Vector`). Later, when an event is generated, an enumeration is used to send the event to each object in the list. Listing 3.5 illustrates how this might be implemented within the `Monitor` class.

**Listing 3.5: A partial** `Monitor` **class**

```java
import java.awt.*;
import java.util.*;

public class Monitor extends Panel {
    private Vector listeners = new Vector();
    ....
    public Monitor() {
        ....
    }
    ....
    public synchronized void addMonitorEventListener(
            MonitorEventListener l) {
        listeners.addElement(l);
    }
    public synchronized void removeMonitorEventListener(
            MonitorEventListener l) {
        listeners.removeElement(l);
    }
    ...
    public void increment() {
        if (count != total)
            count++;
        else {
            MonitorEvent me = new MonitorEvent(this);
            me.setTrigger(count);
            synchronized (this) {
                MonitorEventListener ml;
                Enumeration e = listeners.elements();
                while (e.hasMoreElements()) {
                    ml = (MonitorEventListener)
                                    e.nextElement();
                    ml.monitorEventPerformed(me);
                }
            }
        }
    }
}
```

Note that the enumeration used to send the monitor event to each of
the listeners is wrapped within a synchronized block. This ensures
that the processor cannot interrupt this operation and thus reduces
the chance that something will happen to one of the listener objects
before the event can be sent to it.

# Multicast and Unicast sources

The source of an event can indicate whether it is multicast or unicast.
The examples presented so far have all been multicast. That is, zero

or more objects may act as receivers of an event. A unicast source
object, however, only allows a single object to register as the handler
for an event (at any one time). If more than one object tries to register
as an event handler for a unicast source object then an exception is
raised. This exception is the `java.util.TooManyListeners-`
`Exception`.

## Events and Beans

The next chapter illustrates a concrete example of how events are
used within JavaBeans. Essentially, they are used in exactly the same
way as in the AWT, the only difference being that the developer must
maintain the list of listeners and send the events to the listeners when
appropriate. Of course, the AWT classes do this as well; the
difference is that in the AWT many people do not know what is really
going on but can develop GUI applications. In JavaBeans you do
need to understand what is happening in order to implement your own
bean event sources as well as bean event listeners.

# *4 Building basic beans*

## Introduction

This chapter allows you to actually get your hands dirty and create some simple beans. It therefore explains what you need to do to create a bean as well as the steps to take to allow you to test your bean in the BeanBox.

## Objectives

On completion of this chapter you will be able to:

- Define your own beans.
- Follow the JavaBeans conventions.
- Create a Java Archive (jar) file for your beans.
- Use your beans within the BeanBox.

## The JavaBeans Architecture

A JavaBean is an ordinary Java class that must describe itself following a specified naming convention or by using a `BeanInfo` object. This approach is in contrast with some other component models (notably Delphi's VCL) in which components must inherit from a particular ancestor class. This can be a point of confusion for JavaBean developers, who might well attempt to find the Bean class upon which to construct their bean. Instead, any class in Java can be converted into a Bean as long as it follows the Bean naming conventions or defines a `BeanInfo` object. The only thing to add to this is that if a Bean has a visual appearance which can be used within a tool builder then the Bean must inherit from the AWT class `Component` or one of its subclasses. The great advantage of this approach is its simplicity; the disadvantage is that, at first sight, it appears that there is nothing concrete that defines a bean.

# Creating a Bean

To make a class into a Bean you must follow a set of naming conventions for the methods you define. For example, if you define a property such as `name` (an instance variable holding a single value) then this is indicated by defining `set` and `get` methods (e.g. `setName` and `getName`). If a Bean needs to provide additional information, or does not follow the conventions, then a class implementing the `BeanInfo` interface must be provided. This works in association with the Bean to provide information on its properties, methods and events.

One of the JavaBeans model's greatest strengths is thus its simplicity. In addition, because all that distinguishes a Bean from any other Java class is the naming convention, there is no overhead associated with defining creating, or using a bean.

In the remainder of this chapter we shall review the concept of JavaBeans and then consider how a JavaBean is defined. We shall also examine one particular example of how a simple Java class can be converted into a Bean and used within the Bean Box developer tool.

# The Beans conventions

There are a number of conventions associated with JavaBeans. The first of these was mentioned above and relates to properties; others relate to methods, events, the `BeanInfo` object and the visual representation of beans.

# Properties

To make a private instance variable into a published property *getter* and *setter* methods should be provided which match the following format:

```
public <property type> get<Property Name> ( )
public void set<Property Name> (<property type>
parameter)
```

In addition if the property is a boolean property then by convention this is indicated by `is` followed by the (capitalized) property name, for example:

```
public boolean is<property name>
```

Note that a `get<Property Name>` method should not be defined for a boolean property. The BeanBox does not enforce this; however other bean builders might well. It is therefore best to define `is<Property Name>` and `set<Property Name>` methods for boolean properties.

Properties can be read, read/write or write-only and can be simple, indexed, bound or constrained.

- *Simple* This is the most basic property type and contains a single value. Changes in this value are independent of changes in any other property.
- *Bound* A bound property is one in which a change to the property results in a notification of that change being sent to some other Bean
- *Constrained* A constrained property is one in which an attempt to change the property's value is validated by another Bean. The second Bean may reject the change if it is not acceptable.
- *Indexed* An indexed Bean property is one that supports a range of values instead of a single value (that is, the property is actually an array of values).

Simple will be used in the example presented below. The other types will be discussed later in this chapter.

# Events

Event-handling in JavaBeans is exactly the same as event-handling in JDK 1.1 of the AWT. This means that there are sources of events (in this case Beans), event objects and receivers of events (or listeners). However, JavaBeans imposes some restrictions on the naming of the methods associated with events in order that it can determine the events fired by a Bean automatically. This means that the methods used to register event listeners must match the following conventions:

```
public void add<listener type> (<listener type> listener)
public void remove<listener type> (<listener type>
listener)
```

Note that this assumes that an appropriate listener interface has been defined.

Beans also introduce a number of special events used by the bean mechanism.

If you are unclear on any of the terminology associated with events then you should re-read the previous chapter.

## Methods

Any method that is public, but does not match the above conventions, is assumed to be one that is published by the Bean. Such methods may be called by other beans directly or any Java code. Note that a limitation in the BeanBox used in the example presented below is that it can only deal with public methods that return no value and take no parameters.

## Graphic Beans

Any Bean which has a visual representation that can be used within a Bean development tool, such as the BeanBox, must subclass the `Component` class or one of its subclasses. This will allow it to use the standard AWT facilities to draw itself in the development tool. Note that non-visual beans can also be used in tools such as the BeanBox it is just that they have no appearance.

## `BeanInfo` Object Naming

The `BeanInfo` object, if present, is expected to have a name that matches the following convention:

```
<BeanName>BeanInfo
```

# The BeanInfo Object

A BeanInfo object is an object that provides information on a bean's properties and methods. This can be used if the developer of a bean has not followed the Bean's naming conventions or if the developer wished to provide additional information (for example an icon etc.). BeanInfo is actually an interface that must be implemented by any class providing Bean information. A convenience class, SimpleBeanInfo, defined in the JavaBeans API, provides default implementations for the methods specified in the BeanInfo interface.

In many situations the JavaBeans API can quite adequately provide all the information required by a builder tool. However there a number of situations in which a BeanInfo object can be useful in addition to those mentioned above. The following list indicates situations in which a BeanInfo object can be useful:

- To limit a long list of properties or events.
- To provide an icon for the builder tool's component palette.
- To provide descriptive, human-readable, and possibly localized names for properties.
- To provide facilities for novice and expert operating modes.
- To specify "wizard" style customizers for beans.
- To map a class to the bean naming conventions.

The BeanInfo interface and the SimpleBeanInfo class are discussed in more detail later in the next chapter.

# The Counter and Alarm Beans

The Counter bean is similar to the Monitor described in the last chapter; however, it responds to direct calls to the increment() method rather than to clock tick events (we shall come back to the egg-timer application again later in the book).

## Listing 4.1: The `Counter.java` file

```java
package counter;
import java.awt.*; import java.util.*;

public class Counter extends java.awt.Panel {
    private long count;
    private Vector listeners = new Vector();
    private Label label;
    private long initialValue, maxValue;
    private boolean rollOver = true;

    public Counter() {
        setBackground(Color.blue);
        setForeground(Color.white);
        label = new Label(" ");
        add(label);
    }
    public Dimension getMinimumSize() {
        return new Dimension(30, 30);
    }
    public void setInitialValue(long init) {
        initialValue = init;
    }
    public long getInitialValue () {
        return initialValue;
    }
    public void setMaxValue(long max) {maxValue = max;}
    public long getMaxValue () {return maxValue;}
    public void setRollOver(boolean state) {
        rollOver = state;
    }
    public boolean isRollOver (){return rollOver;}
    public synchronized void addMaxValueListener
                                (MaxValueListener l){
        listeners.addElement(l);
    }
    public synchronized void removeMaxValueListener
                                (MaxValueListener l) {
        listeners.removeElement(l);
    }
    public void reset() {count = initialValue;}
    public void increment() {
        if (count != maxValue) {
            count++;
            label.setText(count + "");
        }
        else {
            if (isRollOver())
                reset();
            else {
                MaxValueEvent mve =
                                new MaxValueEvent(this);
                synchronized (this) {
                    MaxValueListener ml;
                    Enumeration e =
                                listeners.elements();
```

```
                                    while (e.hasMoreElements()) {
                                        ml = (MaxValueListener)
                                                        e.nextElement();
                                        ml.maxValueReached(mve);
                                    }
                                }
                            }
                        }
                    }
                }
```

Listings 4.1 and 4.2 define two simple JavaBeans that are intended to work together. These beans act as a simple counter and a simple alarm. The Counter bean increments a visual counter whenever its increment method is called. When the counter reaches its maximum value, if the rollover property is false, then an event is triggered. This event is sent to a bean (or any Java class) which implements the MaxValueListener interface. When the Alarm bean receives this event it is triggered (which results in its visual representation changing from a white square to a red square).

### Listing 4.2: The Alarm.java file

```java
package counter;
import java.awt.*;
public class Alarm extends Canvas
                    implements MaxValueListener {
    private boolean triggered = false;
    public Alarm () {
        setBackground(Color.white);
    }
    public boolean isTriggered() {return triggered;}
    public void setTriggered(boolean state) {
        triggered = state;
    }
    public Dimension getMinimumSize() {
        return new Dimension(30, 30);
    }
    public void maxValueReached(MaxValueEvent e) {
        setTriggered(true);
        setBackground(Color.red);
    }
}
```

## The Counter Bean

The first Bean, the Counter Bean, counts up to a maximum value and then either resets its counter or notifies an Alarm Bean (via an event), depending on the state of the property `rollOver`, that it has reached its maximum value.

The initial value and the maximum values for the counter are also properties. Notice that the naming conventions imposed by JavaBeans have been followed and thus no `BeanInfo` object is required. We therefore know that the private instance variables `count`, `listeners` and `label` are not properties as they do not have the necessary `get` or `set` methods.

The `increment()` method in the `Counter` Bean is used to increment the value of the `count` instance variable. If this reaches the `maxValue`, the `counter` is either reset or the `MaxValueEvent` is generated. This is then sent to any objects that have registered themselves as a listener of this event with the `Counter`.

The class `Counter` actually extends the class `Panel` in order that the Bean can have a visual representation in a "BeanBox" style tool. `Panel` has been used so that not only can we set the background and foreground colours (features inherited from `Component` via `Panel`), we can also add other components to the display (in this case a simple text label object). This text label will be used to display the current value of the count variable (via the `setText()` method). We have also defined a `getMinimumSize()` method which will be used by a development tool to determine the minimum size to allocate to the visual representation of the Bean. The `Counter` Bean is illustrated pictorially in Figure 4.1.

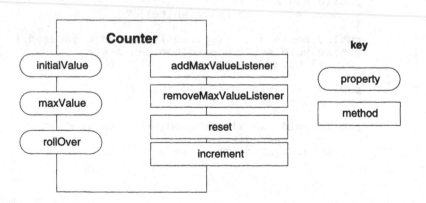

Figure 4.1: The `Counter` Bean

## The Alarm Bean

For the `Alarm` Bean we have sub-classed `Canvas` as we only need to display a coloured square in one of two colours, depending on whether it has been triggered or not. `Triggered` is a property which can either be set via the property tool editor or when the `maxValueReached()` method is executed. The result is that the box displayed by the `Alarm` bean is white when not triggered and red when triggered.

## The `MaxValueEvent` and `MaxValueListener` classes

Listing 4.3: The `MaxValueEvent.java` file

```
package counter;
public class MaxValueEvent extends java.util.EventObject {
    public MaxValueEvent(Object object) {
            super(object);
    }
}
```

Two additional classes are defined in Listings 4.3 and 4.4. These classes are not Beans but are auxiliary classes used by the previous two beans. They define a simple event and an event listener interface. The event class, `MaxValueEvent`, defines the event which will be generated by the `Counter` Bean but caught by the `Alarm` Bean. It extends the `java.util.EventObject` class (as was described in the last chapter, this is the root class of all event classes).

Listing 4.4: The MaxValueListener.java file

```
package counter;
public interface MaxValueListener
                     extends java.util.EventListener {
    void maxValueReached(MaxValueEvent m);
}
```

In turn, the `MaxValueListener` defines an interface which specifies that any object registering itself as a `MaxValueListener` (a receiver of an event) must define the `maxValueReached()` method. For example, the `Alarm` Bean will act as just such a listener for the `Counter` Bean, and therefore it implements the `maxValueReached()` method (see Listing 4.4).

Finally, in order for the `Alarm` Bean to register as a listener with the `Counter` Bean, the `Counter` Bean must define the appropriate `addMaxValueListener()` and `removeMaxValueListener()` methods.

# Packaging the Beans

We are now in a position to package up the two beans (and auxiliary classes) so that they can be used by the BeanBox tool. Remember that the BeanBox tool expects beans to be placed in a JAR file within a directory called `jars` (beans can be loaded from other directories using the **Load Jar** option from the BeanBox **File** menu). A JAR file is a ZIP format archive file with an optional MANIFEST file (JAR stands for Java Archive file). For tools such as the BeanBox the manifest file is required as it provides the BeanBox with information on which files are beans (see Listing 4.5). The statement `Java-Bean: <boolean>` is used to indicate whether the preceding class is a bean or not.

Listing 4.5: The `manifest.tmp` file

```
Name: counter/MaxValueListener.class
Java-Bean: False

Name: counter/MaxValueEvent.class
Java-Bean: False

Name: counter/Counter.class
Java-Bean: True

Name: counter/Alarm.class
Java-Bean: True
```

Constructing the JAR file, and placing the JAR file in an appropriate directory, can be done manually or using a make file. The actual `jar` tool can be used to construct a JAR file for the example classes described above using (note that this assumes the `*.class` files are held in a subdirectory called `counter`):

```
jar cvfm c:\bdk\jars\counter.jar manifest.tmp
counter\*.class
```

The options specify that a new JAR file should be created and the `*.class` files added to it. The first parameter specifies where the JAR file should be placed, the second parameter specifies the name of the manifest file and the third parameter specifies where to look for the files to archive.

# Using the beans

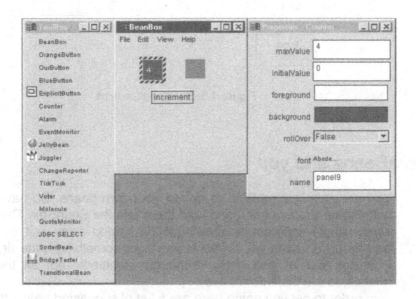

Figure 4.2: The BeanBox with the Counter and Alarm beans

The result of running the BeanBox tool, having created the JAR file, is illustrated in Figure 4.2. As you can see, the two beans have been added to the ToolBox palette. The BeanBox window itself demonstrates the functionality of the two beans. Each bean has been added to the window, and the properties of the Counter bean have been set in the Property Sheet (e.g. the maxValue is 4 and the rollOver property is false). A third bean, an ExplicitButton bean, has been added and used to call the increment() method on the Counter bean (in the same way that the startJuggling and stopJuggling methods were linked to the buttons in Chapter 2). In turn, the Counter bean has been connected to the Alarm bean via the event MaxValueEvent. In the figure, the Counter has reached its maximum value and the event has been sent to the Alarm Bean, which has changed its colour to red (from its default white).

The relationships between the three beans are illustrated graphically in Figure 4.3.

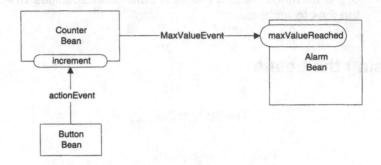

Figure 4.3: Bean relationships

## JavaBeans and you

You are now in a position to define your own beans. So have a go: build some simple beans and load them into the BeanBox. Then build some simple applications. Don't get too carried away, but also don't be afraid to have a go. If you haven't got something quite right, the BeanBox will let you know (although admittedly not all the error messages are that informative).

In order to get you going here are a list of suggested beans that you might like to try implementing:

- A label bean which generates an event each time it is changed.
- A simple editor bean which generates an event when enter is pressed (passing the text entered with the event).
- Circle, square or diamond beans which allow their dimensions to be controlled.
- A random number generator bean (see the static method random() in the class java.lang.Math).
- A graph bean which plots values passed to it on a standard two-dimensional grid (you could allow the scales of the axes to be properties etc.).
- A table bean with rows and columns (including column headings).

You might like to link some of these together. For example, you could define the random number bean to send a number to the graph bean each time a button is pressed. The value sent to the graph bean could then be plotted (e.g. the x scale would represent the number of each value and the y scale the actual value – what happens if a random number outside the specified scale is received?).

# **5** *Property Data Types*

## Introduction

Earlier in this book we said that there were four different types of Bean property: simple, indexed, bound or constrained. So far we have only looked at simple properties. In this section we shall look at the bound, constrained and indexed data types in more detail.

## Objectives

On completion of this chapter you will be able to:

- Define a Bean property of the appropriate type.
- Understand when to use which type of property.
- Use appropriate support classes with bound and constrained properties.

## Simple properties

These are bean properties with a single value in which changes to the value are only of interest to the bean itself (compare this with bound properties). The `Counter` and `Alarm` beans in the last chapter used simple properties. To recap, a property is defined via the set<property name>() and get<property name> methods. If you wish to make a property:

- **read only** You should only provide the get<property name>() method.
- **write only** You should only provide a set<proeprty name>() method.
- **read / write** You must provide both set and get methods.

Note that if a property is a boolean you should provide an is<property name> method instead of a get<property name> method.

# Bound properties

Figure 5.1: The **Edit** menu with **Bind property** option

A bound property is a property that, when changed, results in other beans being informed of the change. This is done by tying the values of a source property and a target property together, such that as the value of one changes so does the second. For example, we can bind the background colour property of an ExplicitButton bean to the background colour of the BeanBox itself. Thus when the background colour of the button is changed the BeanBox will be notified (and in this case will change its background colour to be the same). You can do this because the background colour of a button is a bound property. You can find out whether a bean has any bound properties by selecting it in the BeanBox (so that a hashed boundary is displayed around it) and then selecting the **Edit** menu. If the menu contains the option **Bind property...** then it contains bound

properties. For example, Figure 5.1 illustrates the **Edit** menu for the
ExplicitButton bean.

If you select the **Bind Property...** menu option you will be
presented with a PropertyNameDialog listing the bound properties.
Figure 5.2 illustrates this window for the ExplicitButton bean
(note the label "Select source property"). If you select the background
property then you will be able to bind this property to another bean.

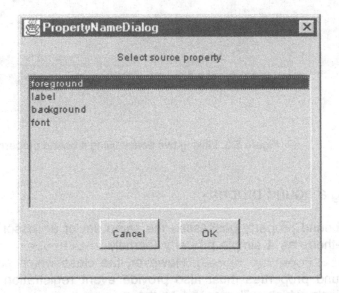

Figure 5.2: The PropertyNameDialog window

Having selected the property to bind, you will find that a red
"rubberband" line is displayed from the ExplicitButton bean to the
cursor. This allows you to connect the selected property to another
bean. In this example we will connect it to the BeanBox itself. You do
this by clicking the mouse on the appropriate bean (in this case
anywhere in the BeanBox window).

Once you have selected another bean a second
PropertyNameDialog is displayed, this time with the label "Select
target property". You can now select the property to change when the
source property changes. In this case, select the background
property.

The BeanBox now creates the linking code required to change the
BeanBox background property when the ExplicitButton's
background property changes.

Next go to the PropertySheet for the ExplicitButton bean and
change the background colour (for example to red). Notice that the

background colour of the BeanBox also changes to red (as illustrated in Figure 5.3).

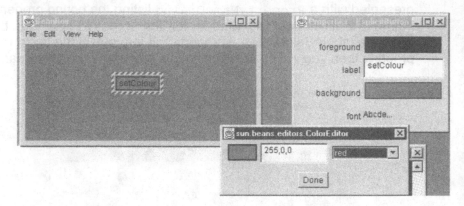

Figure 5.3: Linking two beans using a bound property

## Defining a bound property

A bound property possesses the same set of accessor and updator methods as a simple property (namely `set<Property name>` and `get<Property name>`). However, the class which possesses the bound properties must also provide event registration methods for objects which will respond to the `PropertyChangeEvent`. These objects must implement the `PropertyChangeListener`. This interface defines a single method `propertyChange()` (which takes the `PropertyChangeEvent` as an argument). When the bound property's value is altered each of the objects which has registered itself with the property as a property change listener is sent a property change event by calling its property change method.

To simplify this process the JavaBeans API provides a utility class called `PropertyChangeSupport` that makes the creation of a bound property easier. This class can maintain a list of objects interested in the bound property and can inform these objects of a change in the bound property's value. This is done using the `add/removePropertyChangeListener()` methods and the `firePropertyChange()` method. We shall look at the `PropertyChangeSupport` class in more detail below.

# The `PropertyChangeListener` Interface

The `PropertyChangeListener` interface defines a single method `propertyChange(PropertyChangeEvent)`. Any objects implementing this interface must implement this method. They can then be the recipients of property change events. For example, the `Monitor` class could be extended to implement the `PropertyChangeListener` interface. It could then work with the `Clock` bean defined in the next subsection. For example, see Listing 5.1.

## Listing 5.1: A bound property

```java
import java.beans.*;
import java.awt.*;
import java.util.*;

public class Monitor extends Panel implements
PropertyChangeListener {
    // Non relevant details ommitted
    ...
    // Note that the result of a bound property being
    // changed is that the monitors count value is
    // incremented
    public void propertyChange(PropertyChangeEvent e) {
        increment();
    }
    public void increment() {
        if (count != total)
            count++;
        else {
            MonitorEvent me = new MonitorEvent(this);
            me.setTrigger(count);
            synchronized (this) {
                MonitorEventListener ml;
                Enumeration e =
                            listeners.elements();
                while (e.hasMoreElements()) {
                    ml = (MonitorEventListener)
                                e.nextElement();
                    ml.monitorEventPerformed(me);
                }
            }
        }
    }
}
```

In this version of the `Monitor` class, each time a bound property is changed the Monitor's `count` is incremented. When it reaches a pre-specified total, a `MonitorEvent` will be generated.

## `PropertyChangeSupport` class

This is a support class intended to simplify the production of bound properties. It is provided as part of the JavaBeans API (i.e. the `java.beans` package). It maintains a list of property change listeners and can notify these listeners of a change in a property's value. To use this class all you have to do is provide your own interface to the add and remove `propertyChangeListener()` methods and to call the `firePropertyChange(String, Object, Object)` method at the appropriate times. For example, see Listing 5.2.

### Listing 5.2: Using property change support

```
private PropertyChangeSupport sup =
                        new PropertyChangeSupport(this);
...
// Register PropertyChange listeners
public void
addPropertyChangeListener(PropertyChangeListener l) {
    sup.addPropertyChangeListener(l);
}
public void
removePropertyChangeListener(PropertyChangeListener l) {
    sup.removePropertyChangeListener(l);
}
...
// Within set<property name> method, e.g. setMax(int I)
    sup.firePropertyChange("max",
                        new Integer(oldMax),
                        new Integer(max));
```

Note that the `firePropertyChange()` method takes a string and two objects as parameters. We therefore need to wrap the basic `int` types held by `oldMaxValue` and `maxValue` in integer objects.

## The `Clock` Bean

As an example of a bound property consider the `Clock` bean we described in Chapter 1. This bean needs to inform other beans each time a "tick" occurs. One way of doing this would be to fire an event each time the clock's time field was changed. This could be implemented as a bound property. The code in Listing 5.3 illustrates how this might be done. Note that this bean does not include a way of automatically incrementing the time at specified intervals (e.g. once every second; nor does it worry about there being 60 seconds in a minute), in order to highlight the bound property.

## Listing 5.3: The `Clock` bean

```java
import java.awt.*;
import java.awt.event.*;
import java.beans.*;
public class Clock extends Panel {
    // Internal timer
    private float time = 0.00f;
    private TextField field = new TextField(4);
    // Bound property support
    private PropertyChangeSupport support =
                        new PropertyChangeSupport(this);

    public Clock() {
        add(field);
        field.setText(time + "");
    }

    // Event listener registration methods
    public void addPropertyChangeListener(
                        PropertyChangeListener l) {
        support.addPropertyChangeListener(l);
    }

    public void removePropertyChangeListener(
                        PropertyChangeListener l) {
        support.removePropertyChangeListener(l);
    }

    public float getTime() {
        return time;
    }

    public void increment () {
        float oldTime = time;
        time++;
        field.setText(time + "");
        support.firePropertyChange("time",
                                new Float(oldTime),
                                new Float(time));
    }
}
```

Now that the `time` is a bound value we are in a position to link it to one or more beans that will be notified of a change in its value. For example, if the `Monitor` class is extended as described earlier it can receive notification of the clock's timer property changing.

# Constrained properties

With a constrained property a separate bean validates the changes made. This means that when a change is performed on a constrained property, a separate bean is informed of this change via the event-handling mechanism. This second bean either accepts the change or rejects it. The bean containing the constrained property is responsible for catching any exceptions raised (when the value is rejected) and reverting the property to its previous value. Thus the order in which things happen to a constrained property, within the set<Property name> method, is very important. They must follow this pattern:

- Save the current value of the property.
- Notify listeners of the new value.
- If no listener vetos the change (that is raises an exception), then change the value of the property.

Defining a constrained property is similar to defining a bound property in that you need to register beans that will listen for changes to the property. However, it differs from bound properties in that the listeners may raise a PropertyVetoException. This indicates that the new value has been rejected. This means that the set<Property name> method throws the PropertyVeto--Exception. For example:

```
public void setMaxSize(int s) throws
                        PropertyVetoException{...}
```

The beans that listen for the changes in the constrained property must implement the VetoableChangeListener interface. This interface defines a single method vetoablePropertyChange() which takes a single argument PropertyChangeEvent. This method should check the new value of the property and either raise a PropetyVetoException or return null.

To simplify the maintenance and notification of the listeners the JavaBeans API provides a utility class called VetoableChange-Support. This class defines methods for adding and removing listeners (addVetoableChangeListener() and remove-VetoableChangeListener) and a notification method fireVetoableChange(). As with the bound property, the notification method takes a string (indicating the property that has changed), and two objects that represent the old value of the property and the proposed new value of the property:

```
public void fireVetoableChange(String propetyName, Object
                        oldValue, Object newValue) {..}
```

As an example, consider the partial class definition in Listing 5.4 for a constrained property `maxSize`.

### Listing 5.4: A constrained property

```
public class Square extends Canvas {
    // Set up veto support
    private VetoableChangeSupport vetos =
                        new VetoableChangeSupport(this);
    ...
    // Registration methods for vetos
    public void
      addVetoableChangeListener(VetoableChangeListener l) {
        vetos.addVetoableChangeListener(l);
    }
    public void removeVetoableChangeListener(
                        VetoableChangeListener l) {
        vetos.removeVetoableChangeListener(l);
    }
    public void setMaxSize(int size)
                        throws PropertyVetoException {
        vetos.fireVetoableChange("maxSize",
                        new Integer(maxSize),
                        new Integer(size));
        // no veto - otherwise would have raised exception
        maxSize = size;
        repaint();
    }
}
```

Note that the above approach assumes that the component that requested the bean to change its value (e.g. a property sheet) should be the one to deal with the exception.

An interesting question is what should happen if the bean holding the property wishes to validate changes to that property. It would certainly be possible to register the bean as the listener for its own property. However, this would not be very efficient. It would therefore be better to check the value of the property within the set<Property name> method directly.

As an example of a vetoer, consider the source code for a `SquareVetoer` class in Listing 5.5.

### Listing 5.5: A vetoer class

```
public class SquareVetoer
                implements VetoableChangeListener {
    public void vetoableChange(PropertyChangeEvent e) throws
            PropertyVetoException {
```

```
        int newValue =
            ((Integer)e.getNewValue()).intValue();
        if (newValue > 100)
        throw new PropertyVetoException("Size > 100", e);
    }
}
```

As you can see from the code, the vetoer implements the VetoableChangeListener. Within the vetoableChange() method it checks the new size and raises a PropertyVeto-Exception if the new size is more than 100.

# Indexed properties

In some situations a property actually needs to hold a number of values. In JavaBeans this is achieved using an indexed property which holds an array of values or objects. With an indexed property it is possible to read or write a single element of the array or the whole array. This means that an indexed property is defined by the following get and set methods:

```
public PropertyElement get<Property name>(int index) { ... }
public PropertyElement[] get<Property name>() { ... }
```

and

```
public void set<Property name> (int index, PropertyElement
    element) { ... }
public void set<Property name>(PropertyElement [] elements)
    { ... }
```

It is important to note the differences between the two different types of method. One type deals with an element of the array, the other type with the whole array.

# 6 *Reflection and Bean Introspection*

## Introduction

Some component models require that a component's interface be explicitly defined via some interface definition language. However, JavaBeans merely requires the developer to follow a predefined set of naming conventions and "automagically" the builder tool is informed what properties are available, what methods can be called etc. You may wonder how this is possible. It is actually achieved via a process known as introspection. This chapter considers this process in some detail, primarily so that you understand what happens when a bean is used.

## Objectives

Upon completion of this chapter you will be able to:

- Explain the purpose of introspection.
- Explain the processes involved in introspection.
- Understand the role of the `BeanInfo` object in introspection.
- Explain why the naming conventions in JavaBeans are important.
- Determine what the reflection API does.

# Reflection

The introspection process makes a great deal of use of the reflection API provided with Java (see `java.lang.reflect`) and the `java.lang.Class` class. In this package you will find a selection of classes which have names such as `Method`, `Field`, `Constructor` etc. This may seem strange, as these are the names of elements of a class. Stranger still may appear the `java.lang.Class` class. However, note the capitalization on all these names (they all have a capital letter). They are all therefore classes in their own right. This is because they are used to represent information about a class. Thus the class `Method` contains information about a specific method, such as its name, its parameters and whether it is static or not.

When combined with the facilities defined in the class `java.lang.Class` it is possible to query a class object in order to find out what is defined for that class. Note that we refer here to a class object. This is the object that represents a class. There are two ways in which you can obtain such an object. One is to use the static `forName(String)` method defined in the class `java.lang.Class`. The other is to directly reference the `*.class` file for a class. For example, the following two statements both result in the variable `cls` holding a class object for the class `Clock`.

```
Class cls = Class.forName("Clock");
Class cls = Clock.class;
```

The first version is slightly superior in that it forces the developer to catch the `java.lang.ClassNotFoundException`. This ensures that a program can degrade gracefully.

The reflection facilities are heavily used by the introspection process. This should not cause you concern, as most JavaBeans developers will only need to make the most basic use of the reflection classes.

The class most often used with the introspection process (and `BeanInfo` objects) from the reflection API is the class `Method`.

A `Method` object provides information about, and access to, a single method on a class or interface. The reflected method may be a class method or an instance method (including an abstract method).

It is obtained by first accessing the appropriate class object, and then either using the `getMethod()` method to access a specific method or the `getMethods()` method to obtain an array of all methods defined on the class:

```
public Method getMethod(String, Class[]) throws
NoSuchMethodException, SecurityException
```

> This method returns the Method object for the method specified by the first argument (with the parameters specified by the second argument array). The second argument should be null for a method that takes no arguments.

```
public Method[] getMethods() throws
SecurityException
```

> Returns an array containing Method objects reflecting all the public member methods of the class or interface represented by this Class object, including those declared by the class or interface and those inherited from superclasses and super interfaces. Returns an array of length 0 if the class or interface has no public member methods.

To learn more about the core Reflection API see the java.lang.Class class and the java.lang.reflect package.

# The Introspection process

The introspection process allows a builder tool or a developer to examine the component at run-time to determine how it can interact with other components. The intention is that this minimizes the amount of extra work required by a Bean developer in order to make the Bean available for use by others.

So what is introspection? Put simply, it is the process which queries Beans and BeanInfo objects for the list of properties, methods, events etc. associated with the Bean. To do this, introspection uses reflection and the BeanInfo classes. By combining reflection with a rigid set of naming conventions it is relatively straightforward to determine a bean's details. For example, if a public method with the name setType() is found, then there will be a property type etc.

Introspection is initiated by the getBeanInfo() method of the class Introspector (in the java.beans package). The introspection process follows a detailed plan for filling out what are called Descriptors that describe the properties, events and methods of a Bean.

The actual introspection process has essentially two steps. The first step involves finding a `BeanInfo` object, while the second step relies on filling out any information which has not been provided by the `BeanInfo` object using reflection.

## The `BeanInfo` object

The introspection process first looks for a `BeanInfo` object. If it finds one then it uses this object to fill in as much detail about the bean as possible. This involves retrieving descriptor information used to describe everything from the icon to use with the bean to the properties available. The introspector will identify a class called `MyComponentBeanInfo` as the `BeanInfo` object for the Bean named *MyComponent*.

## Reflection

Secondly, the introspector uses various facilities of the core Reflection API to determine the names of all the methods in any given Bean class. It then applies the naming conventions to determine what properties the Bean has, the events to which it can listen and those that it can send. This illustrates how important the naming conventions are, without which the introspection process would not be able to determine any useful information not provided by the `BeanInfo` object. This would place a far greater burden on the developer.

## The full `BeanInfo` object

Essentially, the process results in a fully filled in `BeanInfo` object. Note that if no `BeanInfo` object has been supplied by the developer the introspector still creates a new one and fills in the details itself.

# How it actually works

The actual steps involved are initiated when the `java.beans.Beans.instantiate()` method loads a Bean. Next a call is made to the method `getBeanInfo()` on the introspector class. This looks for classes whose names look like *BeanName*`BeanInfo`. For example:

```
Counter bean = (Counter) Beans.instantiate(classLoader,
                                            Counter);
Class beanClass = Class.forName("Counter");
BeanInfo beanInfo = Introspector.getBeanInfo(beanClass);
```

Note that the second argument to the `instantiate` method could refer to a serialized file, a class or an applet, depending on how the bean has been packaged. The `instantiate` method will first look for a file called `Counter.ser` and then for a file called `Counter.class`. The call to `getBeanInfo()` then initiates the introspection process.

A note of caution is necessary here. If you are using the BeanBox tool provided with the BDK (up to and including April 1997) then you should be wary of using the `Beans.instantiate()` method to load serialized beans. At present it seems to raise problems with packages and `CLASSPATH`. This may be fixed in future releases of the BDK.

Finally, security applies to the introspection process just as it applies to other aspects of Java. The security manager always has control.

# Experimenting with introspection

If you want to see the results of the introspection process, you can request a report on a bean in the BeanBox. This generates a (partially) formatted and slightly abridged version of the end results of introspection. To do this, first select a bean in the BeanBox (i.e. you should have a hashed border around a bean that you have placed in the drawing area of the BeanBox window). Next go to the **Edit** menu and select the **Report** option. You will then find that a lot of text is printed into the command window from which you initiated the BeanBox. For example, the `Monitor` class developed through this book has been used to generate the following report:

```
CLASS: Monitor

H => Hidden
E => Expert
[ => Indexed Property
* => Default Event or Property

Properties:
    total           long       getTotal/setTotal
    background       class java.awt.Color
                               setBackground/setBackground

Event sets:
```

```
monitorTriggerEventHandler
            addMonitorTriggerEventListener/
            removeMonitorTriggerEventListener
```

Methods:
```
public void Monitor.increment()
```

# 7 *BeanInfo Objects*

## Introduction

This chapter introduces the `BeanInfo` interface, the `Simple-BeanInfo` class and the use of `AdditionalInfo` classes. These are extremely useful in modifying a bean's published protocol, its presentation to a human user and supplying information for builder tools.

## Objectives

On completion of this chapter you will be able to:

- Explain the purpose of the `BeanInfo` interface.
- Subclass the `SimpleBeanInfo` class.
- Implement an `AdditionalInfo` class.
- Use `PropertyDescriptor` classes to control the properties provided by a bean.

## The `java.beans` package

The `java.beans` package possesses many of the classes and interfaces discussed in this chapter. In particular, it contains the classes and interfaces presented in Table 7.1.

Table 7.1: Classes and interfaces in the `java.beans` package

| Classes | Interfaces |
|---|---|
| BeanDescriptor | BeanInfo |
| EventSetDescriptor | PropertyChangeListener |
| FeatureDescriptor | VetoableChangeListener |
| IndexedPropertyDescriptor | |
| MethodDescriptor | **Exceptions** |
| PropertyChangeEvent | IntrospectionException |
| PropertyChangeSupport | PropertyVetoException |
| PropertyDescriptor | |
| SimpleBeanInfo | |
| VetoableChangeSupport | |

# `BeanInfo` Objects

A `BeanInfo` object is an object that works with a JavaBean to provide information about that Bean. It is used to control the published protocol of the Bean. It can therefore be used to limit the properties published by the bean (or to change the label used for a property) and to control which public methods are made available, as well as determining what icon should be used in a bean palette for the bean.

This chapter introduces the `BeanInfo` interface, the `SimpleBeanInfo` class and a simple example of using the `SimpleBeanInfo` class to define a new `BeanInfo` object.

# The `BeanInfo` Interface

The `BeanInfo` interface specifies the methods used by the introspector to obtain information about a bean. If no `BeanInfo` object is provided then the introspector obtains information about a bean using reflection. However, if an object is available that implements the `BeanInfo` interface, then the `BeanInfo` methods are used to provide this information. Note that if a method returns null, then the introspector again falls back on reflection. The methods defined by the `BeanInfo` interface are listed in Table 7.2.

Table 7.2: Methods specified by the `BeanInfo` interface

| | |
|---|---|
| `getAdditionalBeanInfo()` | This method allows a `BeanInfo` object to return an arbitrary collection of other `BeanInfo` objects that provide additional information on the current bean. This means that you can force reflection to provide most of the details, with only a few elements filled in by the additional `BeanInfo`. |
| `getBeanDescriptor()` | This returns a `BeanDescriptor` object that is used to specify a bean's customizer. |
| `getDefaultEventIndex()` | A bean may have a "default" event, which is the event that will most commonly be used by a user. A builder tool to indicate the default event option could use this. |
| `getDefaultPropertyIndex()` | A bean may have a "default" property that is the property, which will most commonly be initially chosen for update by humans who are customizing the bean. |
| `getEventSetDescriptors()` | This returns an array of `EventSetDescriptors`. Each event descriptor controls how a builder tool allows the user to interact with the bean's events. |
| `getIcon(int)` | This method returns an `image` object that can be used to represent the bean in toolboxes, toolbars etc. |
| `getMethodDescriptors()` | This method returns a set of `MethodDescriptors`. |
| `getPropertyDescriptors()` | This method returns an array of `PropertyDescriptors`. Each property descriptor represents special information that the bean provides on a specific property. |

The methods in Table 7.2 allow you to modify every aspect of your bean. For example, the `getPropertyDescriptors()` method allows you to decide which properties will be presented to the user and what label will be associated with those properties. For example, let us assume that we do not want the `Counter` bean to have a property called `maxValue`. Instead we want the property to be called

*Alarm Trigger*. Listing 7.1 (section 7.8) illustrate how a `BeanInfo` object can be used to do this.

# Classes used with `BeanInfo`

As you can see from Table 7.2, most of the methods return instances of classes of the format `<type-of-information>Descriptors`. This can make the `BeanInfo` object seem daunting. However, these classes are, in the main, straightforward. Each of the classes is summarized below:

**BeanDescriptor** A `BeanDescriptor` provides global information about a bean, including its Java class, its displayName, etc.

**EventSetDescriptor** An `EventSetDescriptor` describes a group of events that a given JavaBean fires.

**IndexedPropertyDescriptor** An `IndexedPropertyDescriptor` describes a property that acts like an array and has an indexed read and/or indexed write method to access specific elements of the array.

**MethodDescriptor** A `MethodDescriptor` describes a particular method that a JavaBean supports for external access from other components.

**PropertyDescriptor** A `PropertyDescriptor` describes one property that a JavaBean exports via a pair of accessor methods.

We shall consider the most commonly used of these classes briefly below.

The `FeatureDescriptor` class

The `FeatureDescriptor` class is the root class of all Descriptors. Its subclasses are illustrated in Figure 7.1 and include `MethodDescriptor`, `PropertyDescriptor` and `BeanDescriptor`. It supports some common information that can be set and retrieved for any of its subclass descriptors. For example, it defines the `setDisplayName()` method.

The `FeatureDescriptor` class defines a single constructor:

`public FeatureDescriptor()` You should not normally create instances of the `FeatureDescriptor` class.

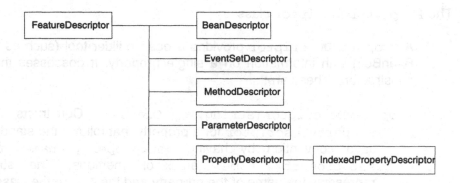

Figure 7.1 : The `FeatureDescriptor` hierarchy

The public methods provided by the `FeatureDescriptor` class are:

`void setDisplayName(String)` **Sets the label used when displaying this property in a property window.**

`void setExpert(boolean)` **The "expert" flag is used to distinguish between features that are intended for expert users from those that are intended for normal users.**

`void setHidden(boolean)` **The "hidden" flag is used to identify features that are intended only for tool use, and which should not be exposed to humans.**

`void setName(String)` **Set the programmatic name of this property (as opposed to the label used when displaying this property to a user).**

`void setShortDescription(String)` **You can associate a short descriptive string with a property.**

`void setValue(String, Object)` **Associate a named attribute with the property receiving this call.**

The `PropertyDescriptor` class

A `PropertyDescriptor` provides a bean builder tool (such as the BeanBox) with information on a single property. It possesses three constructors. These are:

`PropertyDescriptor(String, Class)` Constructs a `PropertyDescriptor` for a property that follows the standard Java convention by having `get<property name>` and `set<property name>` accessor methods. The string represents the name of the property and the `Class` the class of the associated bean. For example, `PropertyDescriptor("maxValue", Counter.class)`.

`PropertyDescriptor(String, Class, String, String)` This constructor takes the name of a simple property and method names for reading and writing the property (defined in the beans class indicated by `Class`).

`PropertyDescriptor(String, Method, Method)` This constructor takes the name of a simple property and method objects for reading and writing the property.

Once a `PropertyDescriptor` has been created you are then in a position to modify information associated with the property. As well as the methods inherited from `FeatureDescriptor`, the `PropertyDescriptor` class provides the following public methods:

`boolean isBound()` Returns true or false depending on whether the property represented by the `PropertyDescriptor` is bound or not.

`boolean isConstrained()` Returns true or false depending on whether the property represented by the `Property-Descriptor` is constrained or not.

`Class getPropertyEditorClass` Returns the `PropertyEditor` class that has been registered for this property. Normally this will return "null", indicating that no special editor has been registered, so the `PropertyEditorManager` should be used to locate a suitable `PropertyEditor` (see Chapter 10).

Class getPropertyType() The Java type information for the property. Note that the Class object may describe a built-in Java type such as int. The result may be null if this is an indexed property that does not support non-indexed access.

Method getReadMethod() This returns the method that should be used to read the property value. May return null if the property cant be read.

Method getWriteMethod() This returns the method that should be used to write the property value. May return null if the property cant be written.

void setBound(boolean) Set whether this property is a bound property or not. This will cause a PropertyChange event to be fired when the property is changed.

void setConstrained(boolean) Set whether this property is a constrained property or not. This will cause a VetoableChange event to be fired when the property is changed.

void setPropertyEditorClass(Class) Normally PropertyEditors will be found using the Property-EditorManager; however you can override that here (see later).

As an example we shall examine the following Java. This short extract uses a PropertyDescriptor object to provide a new label for the property total in the Monitor bean that we have been looking at. This property indicates when the Monitor will trigger a MonitorEvent (for example to the Alarm bean). However, total is not a particularly meaningful name for this value (from the user's point of view). We can therefore provide a label to be used with this property in a PropertySheet:

```
PropertyDescriptor pd;
try {
  pd = new PropertyDescriptor("total", Monitor.class);
  pd.setDisplayName("Monitor Trigger Value");
} catch (IntrospectionException e) {}
```

This short listing provides a property descriptor that adds the label "Monitor Trigger Value" to the `total` property. There are a number of points to note about this:

- The `PropertyDescriptor` constructor we have used takes a `String` and a `Class` object. We can provide a class object in one of two ways. The first is to use the `forName(String)` static method of the class `Class`, for example:

  ```
  Class.forName("Monitor");
  ```

  The second way is to specify the name of the `.class` file. Both will result in an instance of `Class` being returned (see `java.lang.Class`).

- The construction of the `PropertyDescriptor` is placed within a `try{}` `catch{}` block. This is because the `PropertyDescriptor` constructor throws the `java.beans.IntrospectionException` if the specified class does not have the named property. As this class is a subclass of `Exception` it must be handled in some way. The cleanest thing to do is to handle it directly where it is generated (although you may wish to pass the exception up to the builder tool etc.).

## The `MethodDescriptor` class

A method descriptor provides information on a public method published by a JavaBean (see the next chapter for an example). The `MethodDescriptor` class provides two constructors:

`MethodDescriptor(Method)` This creates a method descriptor for the specified `Method` object.

`MethodDescriptor(Method, ParameterDescriptor[])` This creates a method descriptor for the specified `Method` object initialised with information for each of the method's parameters.

See `java.lang.reflect.Method` for more information on the `Method` class. The `MethodDescriptor` only provides two public methods (in addition to those inherited). These are:

`Method getMethod()` This provides a low-level description of the method.

`ParameterDescriptor[] getParameterDescriptors()` **This**
returns an array of `ParameterDescriptors` for the methods
parameters. It may return a null array if the parameter names are
not known.

# The `SimpleBeanInfo` class

The `SimpleBeanInfo` class is a convenience class for the BeanInfo
interface. It provides null implementations for each of the abstract
methods specified in the `BeanInfo` interface.

A developer can either choose to implement the `BeanInfo`
interface or subclass the `SimpleBeanInfo` class. In general, most
developers will subclass `SimpleBeanInfo`. This means that you
only have to implement the methods you are particularly interested in.
This produces more compact and comprehensible code. Note that if,
during introspection, a `BeanInfo` method returns `null`, the
introspector assumes that the `BeanInfo` object does not wish to deal
with this aspect of the bean. The introspector therefore falls back on
reflection to provide details about the bean.

# `AdditionalInfo` Objects

What is an `AdditionalInfo` object? It is a class used in conjunction
with a `BeanInfo` object to combine the results of introspection with
developer–provided bean information. Why is this needed?
Essentially, it is because the introspector described in the last chapter
assumes that if a `BeanInfo` object handles the information about a
particular element of a bean then it handles all the information about
that element. This places an unnecessary burden on the developer.
Consider the following example.

Let us go back to the simple `Counter` bean we defined in Chapter
4. We have decided that the property `maxValue` needs a better label.
If we examine Table 7.2 we can see that the method we need to
define in order to change the label is the
`getPropertyDescriptors()` method. This method returns a
`PropertyDescriptor`. This is a class that can provide information
describing a property. Thus the `getProperty-Descriptors()`
method in Listing 7.1 defines a `PropertyDescriptor` that changes
the label of the `maxValue`.

### Listing 7.1: CounterBeanInfo

```
public class CounterBeanInfo extends SimpleBeanInfo {
    public PropertyDescriptor[]
                getPropertyDescriptors() {
        PropertyDescriptor pd = null;
        // Create a new PropertyDescriptor for MaxValue
        try { pd = new PropertyDescriptor("maxValue",
                                            Counter.class);
        } catch (IntrospectionException e) {}
        pd.setDisplayName("Alarm Trigger");
        PropertyDescriptor result[] = { pd };
        return result;
    }
}
```

Now that we have a `BeanInfo` class for the `Counter` bean, when the introspector attempts to find out the `Counter` bean's details it will load the `CounterBeanInfo` class. It would find that all the methods return null (as they are inherited from `SimpleBeanInfo`) with the exception of the `getPropertyDescriptors()` method. It would therefore use the results obtained from this method to identify the `Counter` bean's properties. Unfortunately, this means that the "Alarm Trigger" property would be the only one presented to the user. This is because the other properties, such as the initial value, were not mentioned by the `getPropertyDescriptors()` method.

Fortunately, this is where the `getAdditionalBeanInfo()` method comes in. Instead of defining the `getProperty-Descriptors()` method in a `CounterBeanInfo` class, you define it in a `CounterAdditionalInfo` class. An instance of this class is then returned by the `getAdditionalBeanInfo()` method defined in the new `CounterBeanInfo` class. The introspector now obtains all the property information for the `Counter` bean by introspection, but replaces the `maxValue` property details provided by reflection with the property details provided by the method in the `CounterAdditionalInfo` class. This is illustrated in Listing 7.2.

### Listing 7.2: Using an AdditionalInfo method

```
public class CounterBeanInfo extends SimpleBeanInfo {
    // Indicates to the introspector to look elsewhere
    // for additional information
    public BeanInfo[] getAdditionalBeanInfo() {
        // Note an array of additional info classes is
        // returned
        return new BeanInfo[] = {
                        new CounterAdditionalInfo() };
```

```
        }
    }

class CounterAdditionalInfo extends SimpleBeanInfo {
    public PropertyDescriptor[]
                               getPropertyDescriptors() {
        PropertyDescriptor pd = null;
        // Create a new PropertyDescriptor for MaxValue
        try { pd = new PropertyDescriptor("maxValue",
                                          Counter.class);
        } catch (IntrospectionException e) {}
        pd.setDisplayName("Alarm Trigger");
        PropertyDescriptor result[] = { pd };
        return result;
    }
}
```

In the above listing we have made the assumption that the AdditionalInfo class is in the same file as the BeanInfo class. There is no need to do this as the additional bean info class can be public (and would thus be defined in its own file).

The result of adding the above BeanInfo classes to the Counter bean (and adding them in the counter.jar file) presented in the last chapter, is illustrated in Figure 7.2.

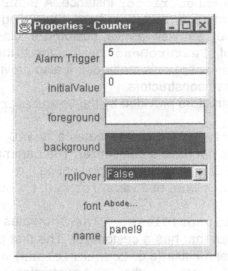

Figure 7:2: The result of applying a BeanInfo class

Note that in order to use the CounterAdditionalInfo class we must add it to the manifest file used with Counter.jar. Therefore our manifest file would look like this:

**Listing 7.3: The manifest file for the** `Counter` **bean**

```
Name: MaxValueListener.class
Java-Bean: False

Name: MaxValueEvent.class
Java-Bean: False

Name: CounterBeanInfo.class
Java-Bean: False

Name: CounterAdditionalInfo.class
Java-Bean: False

Name: Counter.class
Java-Bean: True

Name: Alarm.class
Java-Bean: True
```

# The `getBeanDescriptor` method

The `getBeanDescriptor()` method of the `BeanInfo` interface
returns a `BeanDescriptor` instance. A `BeanDescriptor` provides
global information about a bean, including its Java class, its
displayName, as well as its customizer class. It is yet another
subclass of `FeatureDescriptor` (and thus it inherits all of
`FeatureDescriptor`'s methods). It also provides two new methods
along with two constructors.

The constructors provided by the `BeanDescriptor` class are:

`BeanDescriptor(Class)` creates a `BeanDescriptor` for a bean
that does not have a customizer. The parameter to this constructor
is a `Class` object representing a bean (for example
`Counter.class` or `Class.forName("Counter")`).

`BeanDescriptor(Class, Class)` creates a `BeanDescriptor`
for a bean that has a customizer. The first parameter is the name
of the bean class (e.g. `Counter.class`) while the second is the
name of the customizer class (e.g.
`CounterCustomizer.class`).

The two methods provided by the `BeanDescriptor` class are:

`Class getBeanClass()`  This returns the `Class` object for the bean.

`Class getCustomizerClass()` This returns the `Class` object for the bean's customizer (or null if no customizer has been specified).

A `BeanDescriptor` object, returned by the `getBeanDescriptor()` method, is usually used to specify a customizer to be used with a bean. For example, the `ExplicitButton` bean implements this method in the following manner:

```
public BeanDescriptor getBeanDescriptor() {
        return new BeanDescriptor(beanClass,
                                  customizerClass);
}
```

The `beanClass` and `customizerClass` variables are defined to return the appropriate class objects. We will look again at `BeanDescriptor`s when we consider customizers in Chapter 10.

# *8* *An Example*

# *BeanInfo Object*

## Introduction

This chapter provides a detailed worked example of a `BeanInfo` object for a complete bean. The bean used is the `Clock` bean originally introduced in Chapter 1. We want this `BeanInfo` object to provide a nice clock icon for use in the ToolBox palette. We therefore need to implement the `getIcon()` method. We also want this `BeanInfo` object to change the label used with the `time` property. Instead of `time` we want a more meaningful name such as "Start Time".

   To provide an icon for the clock and to manage the properties and their names we need to implement `ClockBeanInfo` and `ClockAdditionalInfo` classes (remember that if we only had a `ClockBeanInfo` class we would need to specify every single property we want the user to be able to change). Both these classes are subclasses of `SimpleBeanInfo` so that we do not have to provide implementations for each of the `BeanInfo` methods.

## Objectives

Once you have finished this chapter you will be able to:

- Define `BeanInfo` objects.

- Implement getPropertyDescriptors() methods.
- Provide a bean with an icon.
- Control which methods are published

# The Clock bean

We will first look at the Clock bean. This has been extended slightly from the version presented earlier in the book in order to include an interval property (partly to make the bean more reusable and partly to make it more interesting). The Clock class is presented in Listing 8.1.

Listing 8.1: The Clock bean

```java
import java.awt.*;
import java.awt.event.*;
import java.beans.*;

public class Clock extends Panel
                     implements Runnable{
   // Internal time
   private float time = 0.00f;
   private int interval = 1;
   private TextField field = new TextField(4);
   private Thread thread;
   private boolean running = false;
   // Bound property support
   private PropertyChangeSupport support =
                  new PropertyChangeSupport(this);

   public Clock() {
      add(field);
      field.setText(time + "");
      thread = new Thread(this);
   }

   // Event listener registration methods
   public void addPropertyChangeListener(
                       PropertyChangeListener l) {
      support.addPropertyChangeListener(l);
   }

   public void removePropertyChangeListener(
                       PropertyChangeListener l) {
```

```
                        support.removePropertyChangeListener(l);
                }

                public void setInterval(int i) {
                    interval = i;
                }

                public int getInterval() {
                    return interval;
                }

                public float getTime() {
                    return time;
                }

                public void setTime(float f) {
                    time = f;
                }

                public void start() {
                    if (!running) {
                        thread.start();
                        running = true;
                    }
                }

                public void increment () {
                    float oldTime = time;
                    time = time + interval;
                    field.setText(time + "");
                    support.firePropertyChange("time",
                                                 new Float(oldTime),
                                                 new Float(time));
                }

                public void run() {
                    try {
                        thread.sleep(interval * 1000);
                        while (true) {
                            increment();
                            thread.sleep(interval * 1000);
                        }
                    } catch (InterruptedException e) {}
                }

                public static void main (String args []) {
                    Clock c = new Clock();
```

```
      , c.start();
   }
}
```

The primary changes affecting the bean properties are that the `interval` property has been added and that the `time` property is now a read/write property (it has both `set` and `get` methods). The result of using this bean in the BeanBox is illustrated in Figure 8.1.

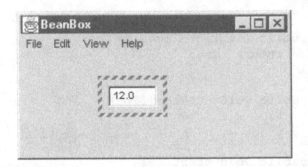

Figure 8.1: Using the Clock bean in the BeanBox

The other additions to the bean allow it to be started and to increment its time property once each second. This is done by creating a `Thread` object, which is a lightweight process. This thread can execute independently. It will execute the method `run()` of any object implementing the `Runnable` interface. Note that the `Clock` class now implements the `Runnable` interface and defines a method `run`. This method forces the thread to continuously sleep, and then increment the `time`, and then sleep, followed by incrementing the `time` etc. The result is that the `time` property is incremented each time the thread wakes up. Note that the thread does not start executing when it is created. Instead, it waits until it is started. This is done when the `start()` method is executed. This is the method which another bean is intended to call (see the `BeanInfoObject`).

## The `ClockBeanInfo` class

The `BeanInfo` class for the `Clock` bean is presented in Listing 8.2. This class is a subclass of `SimpleBeanInfo`. It specifies the icon to use in the ToolBox palette, which properties should be presented to the user (and what they should be called) and which methods are available from the `Clock`. These last two are important issues, as the

`Clock` **extends the** `Panel` **class. It therefore inherits all the variables and methods defined by the class** `Panel` **and its superclasses (which are** `Container`, `Component` **and** `Object`**). Thus if we did not control the bean's published protocol we would have a longer (less meaningful) list of properties and a very long list of public methods.**

**There are three methods defined by the** `ClockBeanInfo` **class, these are** `getIcon()`, `getPropertyDescriptors()` **and** `get-MethodDescriptors()`**. We shall look at each in greater detail after the listing.**

**You might also note that we have defined a private variable** `beanClass`**. This holds an instance of the** `Clock` **class object. This is used in both the** `getPropertyDescriptors()` **and** `getMethodDescriptors()` **methods. It saves specifying the** `Clock` **class object each time and leads to more readable code.**

### Listing 8.2: The `ClockBeanInfo` class

```
import java.beans.*;
import java.awt.Image;
import java.lang.reflect.*;

public class ClockBeanInfo extends SimpleBeanInfo {
  private final static Class beanClass = Clock.class;

  public Image getIcon(int iconKind) {
    Image img = null;
    if (iconKind == BeanInfo.ICON_MONO_16x16 ||
        iconKind == BeanInfo.ICON_COLOR_16x16 ) {
      img = loadImage("Clock16.gif");
    } else if (iconKind == BeanInfo.ICON_MONO_32x32 ||
        iconKind == BeanInfo.ICON_COLOR_32x32 ) {
      img = loadImage("Clock32.gif");
    }
    return img;
  }

  public PropertyDescriptor[] getPropertyDescriptors() {
    PropertyDescriptor time = null,
                       background = null,
                       interval = null;
    // Create a new PropertyDescriptor for MaxValue
    try {
      time = new PropertyDescriptor("time", beanClass);
      time.setDisplayName("Start Time");
      time.setBound(true);
      background = new PropertyDescriptor("background",
                                          beanClass);
      background.setDisplayName("Colour");
      interval = new PropertyDescriptor("interval",
                                        beanClass);
    } catch (IntrospectionException e) {
```

```
        throw new Error(e.toString());
    }
    PropertyDescriptor result[] = { time,
                                    background,
                                    interval };
    return result;
}

    public MethodDescriptor [] getMethodDescriptors() {
        // First find the "method" object.
        Method method = null;
        MethodDescriptor result[] =
                                new MethodDescriptor[1];
        try {
          method = beanClass.getMethod("start", null);
          result[0] = new MethodDescriptor(method);
        } catch (Exception ex) {
          throw new Error("Missing method: " + ex);
        }
        return result;
    }
}
```

Note that this version of the Clock bean makes the start()
method the only published method.

# The getIcon() method

The getIcon(int) method indicates the icon(s) to use in the
ToolBox palette for a bean. By default this method returns null,
indicating that there are no icons. However, you can override the
default implementation inherited from SimpleBeanInfo to return
your own icons. For the Clock bean we are going to provide two
different icons to be used depending upon whether a 16 x 16 or 32 x
32 pixel icon is required. The parameter passed to the
getIcon(int) method indicates the type of icon requested. At
present there are four different types of icon that can be specified:

- **16x16 colour** Indicated by the BeanInfo static variable
  ICON_COLOR_16x16      (access     by     BeanInfo.
  ICON_COLOR_16x16).
- **32x32 colour** Indicated by the BeanInfo static variable
  ICON_COLOR_32x32.
- **16x16 mono** Indicated by the BeanInfo static variable
  ICON_MONO_16x16.
- **32x32 mono** Indicated by the BeanInfo static variable
  ICON_MONO_32x32.

At present, if you only intend to supply one type of icon it is recommended that you supply a 16 x 16 colour icon of pixels in size.

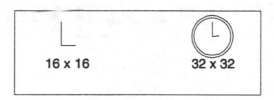

Figure 8.2: The clock icons

For the Clock bean we are providing two icons, one of 16 by 16 pixels and the other of 32 x 32 pixels. The two icons are illustrated in Figure 8.2. These icons are in GIF format. It is not clear what other formats can be used as the JavaBeans documentation states "Icon images will typically be GIFs, but may in future include other formats". This seems to imply that other formats are supported, but no statement is made about which ones.

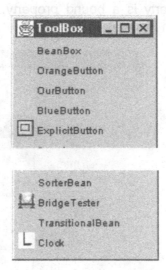

Figure 8.3: The ToolBox palette with the Clock bean icon

The result of adding these icons to the Clock bean is illustrated in Figure 8.3. This figure illustrates part of the ToolBox palette (with the middle cut out). The Clock bean is presented at the bottom of the palette with the 16 x 16 icon.

# The `getPropertyDescriptors()` method

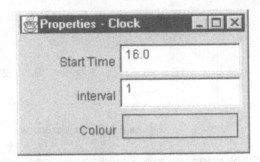

Figure 8.4: The `Clock` PropertySheet

This method is essentially the same as that used by the original `CounterBeanInfo` object except that we have defined three instances of the `PropertyDescriptor` class for the properties `interval`, `background` and `time`. We have also specified that the `time` property is a bound property. The results of doing this are illustrated in Figure 8.4.

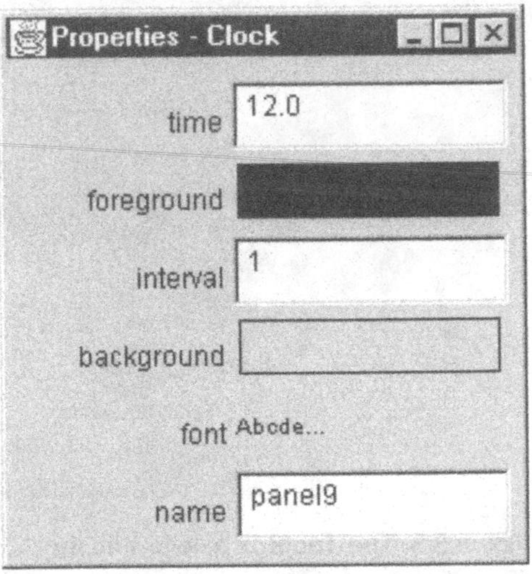

Figure 8.5: The default `Clock` PropertySheet

As you can see from Figure 8.4 using the `propertyDescriptor` class can result in a far more meaningful interface. For example, compare this figure with the default `Clock` PropertySheet (illustrated in Figure 8.5).

## The `getMethodDescriptors()` method

The `Clock` bean at present relies upon an external source to execute the `increment()` method during each interval. This could be a separate bean raising an event at the appropriate times (or a thread running with the `Clock` bean). For testing purposes this type of bean can be simulated using an `ExplicitButton` bean. The user can click on the button to cause the clock to be incremented.

The problem with this sort of interaction between beans, at least from the users' perspective, is that when they try to tie an event raised by one bean with a method on another bean, they are presented with a plethora of methods (particularly if a bean is a graphical bean and thus inherits from a graphical component). For example, Figure 8.6 illustrates the default list of methods presented by the EventTargetDialog window for the `Clock` bean (remember that it inherits from `Panel`, `Container`, `Component` and `Object`).

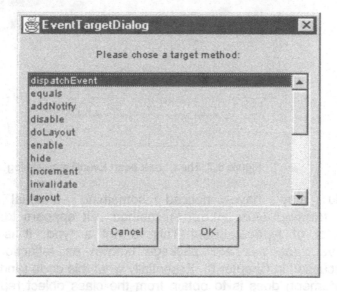

Figure 8.6: The default EventTargetDialog window for the `Clock` bean

As you can see from Figure 8.6, there are very many methods listed (22 in fact). Most of these methods are not relevant to the operation of the `Clock` bean itself (e.g. `doLayout`). Some look as though they might be (such as `disable`, `enable`), yet only one is actually the intended target of an event for the `Clock` bean (that is, the method `start`).

In fact we can make the users' task easier by providing a `getMethodDescriptors()` method. In Listing 8.2 we did exactly that. This method returns `MethodDescriptors` for each of the methods that should be published by the `Clock` bean. In fact there is only one, the `start()` method. Therefore only a single `MethodDescriptor` is returned. The result of this is illustrated in Figure 8.7. This makes it clear to users which method they should link the event to (as there is only one!).

Figure 8.7: The `Clock` bean EventTargetDialog

You may have noticed something unusual about the `getMethodDescriptors()` method – it appears to be using an object of type `Method`! This is not a typo: it is part of the `java.lang.reflect` package (known as reflection and briefly discussed in Chapter 6). Essentially what this code (and the following statement) does is to obtain from the class object representing the `Clock` a method which represents information about the method increment.

```
Method method = beanClass.getMethod("start", null);
```

The `getMethod(string, Class[])` is defined on the class `java.lang.reflect.Method`. It takes two parameters: a `string` representing the name of the method to be accessed and an array of the class of the parameters it takes. As `start()` takes no

parameters we pass in the `null` value. If we needed to obtain a
`Method` object for a method which took one or more parameters we
would have to provide an array contain the appropriate class objects.
For example, if we wished to obtain a method object for a method
`add(String)`, then we would write:

```
Method method = beanClass.getMethod("add",
                                {java.lang.String.class});
```

Don't worry if you find this confusing (the terminology used does not
help – "a method object for the required method"); treat it like an idiom
that you must use and you will probably be okay.

# Handling bound properties

The `Clock` bean now provides a bound property `time`. This property
will notify any beans listening for changes in its value. However, how
do we define a bean that can receive such notification? There are two
ways in which this can be done.

The first, and simplest, way is to tie the value held in the bound
property to a property of the same type on another bean. This is done
from the **Bind Property...** option on the **Edit** menu. If you select the
`Clock` bean and bring up the this menu option you will be presented
with a PropertyNameDialog box for the source property (on the
`Clock` bean). Once you have selected the bound property to use (in
the `Clock` bean there is only one) you can then select the target
property on another bean. Then as the value of the `timer` property
changes, the target property will also have its value changed. This
was done back in Chapter 2 with the background colour of an
`ExplicitButton` bean and the background colour of the BeanBox
itself.

The second, slightly more complex, way is to define a bean which
implements the `PropertyChangeListener` interface. Such a bean
will be notified of changes in the source property by being sent
`PropertyChangeEvents`. You may have noticed that the `Clock`
bean includes an extra entry on the **Events** submenu of the **Edit**
menu. This submenu lists the events currently available from the
`Clock` bean. One of these events is now the `PropertyChange`
event. You can thus select this event and link it to a target bean. This
is the approach taken in the simple egg-timer application being built.
We have therefore extended the `Monitor` class to implement the
`PropertyChange` listener.

The relevant parts of the `Monitor` class definition are presented in Listing 8.3. As you can see from this listing, the key changes are the addition of the `propertyChange(PropertyChangeEvent)` method necessitated by implementing the `ProeprtyChangeListener` interface. In this case the `propertyChange()` method calls the `start()` method, which increments the `monitors` internal counter. No other changes are required.

Listing 8.3: Extending the `Monitor` bean to handle change events

```
import java.beans.*;
import java.awt.*;
import java.util.*;

public class Monitor extends Panel
                  implements PropertyChangeListener {
    ...
    public Monitor() {
        ...
    }
    ...
    public void propertyChange(
                        PropertyChangeEvent event) {
        increment();
    }
    public void increment() {
        ...
    }
}
```

As you can see from this listing, extending a bean to handle notification of changes to bound properties is trivial.

## The manifest and JAR files

We have done almost everything we need to do to make our modified `Clock` bean available to the BeanBox. However, we still need to package the bean (and its associated classes and GIF files) into a JAR file. To do this we must first define a `manifest` file. The `manifest` file for the beans we are defining is presented in listing 8.4.

Listing 8.4: The `Clock` manifest file

```
Name: ClockBeanInfo.class
Java-Bean: False
```

```
Name: Clock16.gif
Java-Bean: False

Name: Clock32.gif
Java-Bean: False

Name: Clock.class
Java-Bean: True
```

Once this file has been written you can jar the bean and its associated files. This is done using the `jar` command you saw earlier in the book. For example:

```
C:\beans>jar cvfm Clock.jar Manifest.tmp *.class *.gif
```

This produces a `Clock.jar` file that we can now load into the BeanBox using the **LoadJar** option on the **File** menu. Alternatively, we could copy the `Clock.jar` file into the `jar` directory under the BDK. This would ensure that each time we start up the BeanBox the `Clock` bean would be available on the ToolBox palette.
ToolBox palette.

# 9 *Bean Serialization*

## Introduction

In some situations it is desirable to save the state of a bean instance. For example, once we have set the properties on a `Counter` bean (for example by setting the `Alarm` bean message to "Egg-Timer" and providing a new icon for the `Alarm` bean) we might want to reuse this configuration many times. We do not want to have to reset the `Alarm` bean's properties every time. So how do we manage this (remember that if you have purchased a bean from a bean vendor, you may not have access to its source code)? In JavaBeans this is achieved by serializing the bean; that is, storing the bean to a file in a format which allows it to be restored at a later stage. This chapter explains the concept of serialization and illustrates how it can be used with JavaBeans.

## Objectives

Once you have finished this chapter you will be able to:

- Explain how serialization works in Java.
- Use serialization to save and restore a bean.
- Implement a bean so that it can be serialized.

# Serialization in Java

Serialization allows you to store objects directly to a file in a compact and encoded form. You do not need to convert the objects or reconstruct them when you load them back in. In addition, everyone else who uses serialization can read and write your files. This is useful not only for portability but also for sharing objects.

The name, serialization, comes from the way in which references between objects saved to a file are maintained. For example, let us assume that we are serializing four objects. Three of the objects reference the fourth. It would not be efficient to save the first three objects, each with their own copy of the fourth. Instead, each object is given a serial number that is used in its place if other objects reference it. This serial number is then used to reconstruct the object structure when it is loaded back into memory.

Any class whose objects are to be used as part of a serializable application must implement the `java.io.Serializable` interface (or the `java.io.Externalizable` interface). If you examine many of the classes provided with the JDK (such as `Vector`) you will find that they already implement the `Serializable` interface. The `serializable` interface acts like a flag indicating to the Java Virtual Machine (JVM) that the associated class can be serialized.

If you define your own classes, then as long as they implement the `Serializable` interface then can also be serialized. As the `Serializable` interface does not require you to implement any method (i.e. it is empty) you can create a serializable class without the need to define any new methods. All the instance variables of an object are written out to the file automatically. When the object is restored the instance variable information is automatically restored.

To serialize an object you need to use an `ObjectOutputStream` linked to a file. The object is then written onto this stream. The data is then passed to the file, via a `FileOutputStream`, in the appropriate format. When an object is de-serialized (read back in from a file), an `ObjectInputStream` is used. The following subsections briefly explain this process. If you are unclear about the use of streams in Java see an introductory Java book (such as J. E. Hunt, *Java and Object Orientation: An Introduction*, Springer-Verlag, 3-540-76201-9, 1998).

## Saving Objects

To save an object to file, you use the `ObjectOutputStream` class. However, an `ObjectOutputStream` must use a stream, such as `FileOutputStream`, to write data to a file:

```
try{
    FileOutputStream file = new FileOutputStream("data");
    ObjectOutputStream output =
                    new ObjectOutputStream(file);
    output.writeObject(vector);
    output.close();
} catch (IOException e) {}
```

The above code results in all the objects held by `vector` being saved to the file `data` using serialization. This illustrates that, although you may find the concepts confusing, serialization is easy to work with.

## Reading Objects

To read objects that have been saved to a serialization file back into an application, you need to use the `ObjectInputStream` class. You must also use an input stream, such as `FileInputStream`, to read the (byte) data from the file:

```
try {
    FileInputStream file = new FileInputStream("data");
    ObjectInputStream input = new ObjectInputStream(file);
    Vector vector = (Vector) input.readObject();
    input.close();
} catch (IoException e) {}
```

Notice that you must cast the object retrieved by the `readObject` method into the appropriate class.

## The `ObjectOutputStream` class

The `ObjectOutputStream` class defines a single constructor that creates an `ObjectOutputStream` that writes to the specified `OutputStream`:

```
ObjectOutputStream(OutputStream)
                            throws IOException
```

## The `ObjectInputStream` class

The `ObjectInputStream` class defines a single constructor that creates an `ObjectInputStream` that reads from the specified `InputStream`:

```
ObjectInputStream(InputStream)
        throws IOException, StreamCorruptedException
```

# Serializing a bean

To serialize a bean you use the **SerializeComponent** menu item from the **File** menu (Figure 9.1). This menu option allows you to write the currently selected bean object to a file. Thus you must have at least one bean object in the BeanBox drawing area and this must be selected (indicated by a hashed line around the bean).

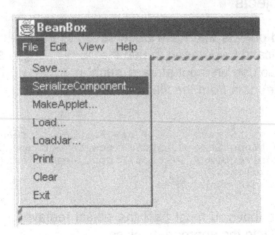

Figure 9.1: The **SerializeComponent** option on the **File** menu

We shall use the `Alarm` bean as an example of why we might want to do this and of how we do it. By default the `Alarm` bean, when triggered, looks like the display presented in Figure 9.2. This is quite acceptable for an alarm clock application. However, for an egg-timer it would be much better to change the label displayed by the `Alarm` bean as well as the icon. These are trivial tasks to perform, as the label and the icon can both be changed using the PropertySheet window. For example, the label could be changed to "Egg is Ready" and the icon to one representing an egg-timer, as illustrated in Figure 9.3.

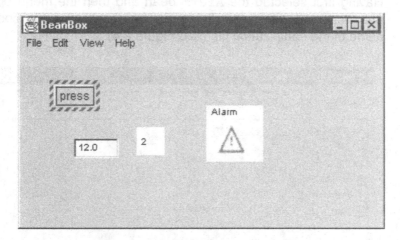

Figure 9.2: The triggered default `Alarm` bean

The problem with this approach is that each time we want to use the egg-timer application with our customized `Alarm` bean we will need to reset the properties of the `Alarm` bean. This is not only tedious but error-prone. Indeed, if we wanted to give our customized bean to others to use, it would be problematic.

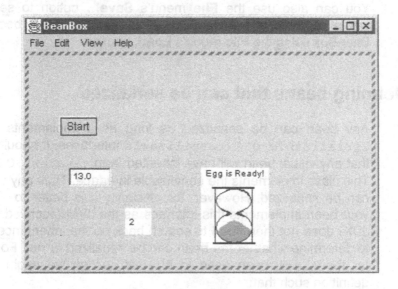

Figure 9.3: Using the customized `Alarm` bean

However, we can use the **SerializeComponent** menu option to save
the state of our `egg-timer Alarm` bean to a file for future use.
Having first selected the `Alarm` bean and then the menu option we
are presented with a file dialog box which allows us to specify the
name of the serialization file (see Figure 9.4).

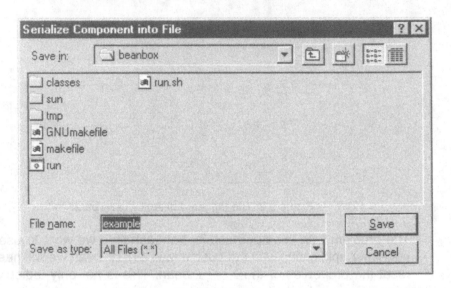

Figure 9.4: The bean serialization file dialog

You can also use the **File** menu's **Save...** option to serialize the
whole contents of the BeanBox. This can be loaded back into the
BeanBox using the **File** menu's **Load...** option.

## Defining beans that can be serialized

Any bean can be serialized as long as it implements either the
`Serializable` or `Externalizable` interfaces. It should be noted
that any visual bean will have inherited from `java.awt.Component`.
This class implements the serializable interface. Thus any visual bean
can be serialized. However, for efficiency it is better to specify that
your bean implements this interface as the JVM (supplied with Sun's
JDK) does not then need to search back up the inheritance hierarchy
to determine whether the bean can be serialized or not. For example,
for the `Alarm` bean used in the last section we might modify its
definition such that:

```
import java.awt.*;
```

```java
import java.awt.image.*;
import java.io.Serializable;

public class Alarm extends Panel
            implements MonitorTriggerEventListener,
                       ImageObserver,
                       Serializable {
  private boolean triggered = false;
  private String imageFile =
                   "c:/jjh/Java/Clock/Alarm32.gif",
                message = "Alarm";
  private Image image;
  public Alarm() {
     setBackground(Color.white);
     // Load the image to use with the alarm. This is
     // done in a platform independent manner using the
     // current toolkit.
     loadImage();
  }
  private void loadImage() {
     try {
       Toolkit toolkit = Toolkit.getDefaultToolkit();
       image = toolkit.getImage(imageFile);
     } catch(Exception e) {
       System.out.println("Problem loading image");
     }
  }
  public void monitorTriggerEventHandler(
                          MonitorTriggerEvent event){
     triggerAlarm();
  }
  public boolean isTriggered() {
     return triggered;
  }
  public void setMessage(String message) {
     this.message = message;
  }
  public String getMessage() {
     return message;
  }
  public void setImageFile(String file) {
     imageFile = file;
     loadImage();
  }
  public String getImageFile() {
     return imageFile;
  }
  public Dimension getMinimumSize() {
     return new Dimension(60, 60);
  }
  public Dimension getPreferredSize() {
     return new Dimension(60, 60);
  }
  public void triggerAlarm() {
     triggered = true;
     repaint();
  }
```

```java
    public void paint (Graphics gc) {
      if (isTriggered()) {
        gc.drawString(message, 5, 10);
        // Note drawImage returns immediately.
        // An image observer is required to determine
        // when the image has been fully loaded (see
        // imageUpdate().
        gc.drawImage(image, 10, 20, this);
      }
    }
    /**
     * This method is used to determine whether the
     * image being displayed has been fully loaded or
     * not. If it returns true then the image still
     * requires more information. If it returns false
     * then the image has been successfully loaded
     * or an error has occurred.
     */
    public boolean imageUpdate(Image img,
                                int infoflags,
                                int x,
                                int y,
                                int width,
                                int height) {

      if (ImageObserver.PROPERTIES == infoflags)
        return true;
      else if (ImageObserver.ERROR == infoflags) {
        System.out.println(
            "Error in image - image display aborted");
        return false;
      } else {
        return true;
      }
    }
  }
```

# *10* Property Editors and Customizers

## Introduction

In this chapter we consider how you can define your own editors for individual properties. We also look at how a "wizard"-style customizer can be provided for a whole bean.

## Objectives

On completion of this chapter you will be able to:

- Explain the difference between a property sheet, a property view, a property editor and a customizer.
- Explain how a property editor and its view are selected.
- Define new property editors.
- Describe how a customizer is selected.
- Implement a customizer.

# Changing property values

We have already seen numerous times how a property's value can be changed using the fields in the PropertySheet window. We have also seen how the labels associated with these fields can be altered so that they present a more meaningful (and potentially localized) interface to the user. However, we can also control how the property values are changed and displayed. That is, we can define how a colour is displayed, how a string is edited or how a property with four values is modified. This can greatly enhance the interface between the user and the bean, thus making it easier for the bean to be used.

# The Property Sheet

The PropertySheet window contains two columns; one for labels indicating the properties concerned and one for the fields that allow the properties value to be changed. An example PropertySheet window is presented in Figure 10.1. The fields on the right of the window provide various "editors" for strings, integers, booleans etc. More complex properties, such as colours, provide separate pop-up windows that allow more complex selections. This is illustrated in the figure for the background colour property. Here the colour editor has been popped up so that a new colour can be specified. These "editors" are referred to as *property editors*.

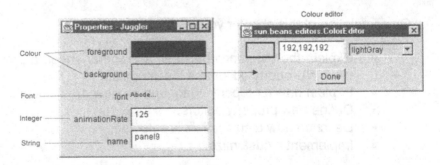

Figure 10.1: The PropertySheet window

The property editors are displayed within different types of views. For example, the colour property editor is displayed within a `PropertyCanvas` view, while the Boolean editor is displayed within a `PropertySelector` view and a string editor is displayed within a

`PropertyText` view. Thus a PropertySheet is made up of labels (for the names of the properties) and property views containing property editors.

Although there are a number of property editors defined by the JavaBeans API, in some situations you will want to be able to provide a property editor with a specific function. For example, you might want to provide a "days of the working week" property editor which allows a user to select from a list of values such as Monday through to Friday (and no other values). You can do this either by implementing the `PropertyEditor` interface or subclassing the `PropertyEditorSupport` class.

In extreme circumstances you may wish to provide greater support than can be achieved using a property editor (for example, to create a "wizard"-style of interface). Thus can be done using customizers which act as standalone interfaces, and which are triggered from the **Customize...** option on the **Edit** menu.

# Property Views

The PropertySheet window determines which property view to use based on which type of editor is associated with a property. This may be determined by the `BeanInfo` object or it may be determined by identifying the type of the property and then looking for a property editor called `<type>editor`. Once the property editor is identified its view can be determined.

Figure 10.2 illustrates the views used with the properties associated with the `Juggler` bean.

To determine which view to use, the property sheet checks the methods defined for the property editor associated with the property:

- The `PropertyCanvas` view is used if the associated property editor defines `isPaintable()` and `supportsCustom-Editor()` as non-null.
- The `PropertySelector` view is used if the property editor defines `getTags()` as non-null and the `getAsText()` method returns a non-null string.
- The `PropertyText` view is used if the property editor defines `getAsText()` as non-null.

The property sheet checks for these methods in the order presented above. The first methods satisfied specify the view that will be used.

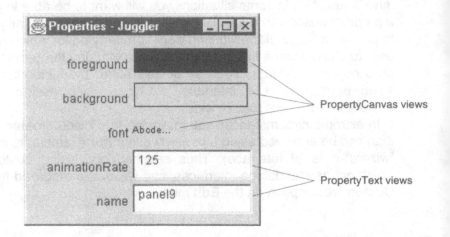

Figure 10.2: Property views used with the `Juggler` PropertySheet window

The `PropertyCanvas` view (illustrated in Figure 10.2) uses a `Canvas` that displays a `Dialog` window when the mouse is clicked on the view (see Figure 10.1). The `PropertySelector` view uses a `Choice` component that presents two or more options to the user. This is used with boolean values. It is also used in the Monitor example presented later in this chapter. The `PropertySelector` view implements the `ItemListener` interface. This means that when an item is selected from the list presented. The `itemState-Changed(ItemEvent)` method is executed. This then passes this information back to the property editor that can update the appropriate property.

Finally, the `PropertyText` view uses a `TextField` to allow strings to be input. Again this is illustrated in Figure 10.2. When new text is typed into the `PropertyText` view the `keyReleased()` method of the `KeyListener` interface. In this way, each time a change is made to the text in the view it can be reported back to the bean represented by the properties (for example, if you provide a new label for an `ExplicitButton` you will notice that the label appears on the button bean immediately).

# Property Editors

A number of built-in property editors are provided by the JavaBeans API (see the `apis\sub\beans\editors\` directory under the BDK directory). Table 10.1 lists the full set of editors provided by JavaBeans. These editors are already registered with the `PropertyEditorManager` (see `java.beans.PropertyEditor-Manager`) and are therefore available for use. The property editor maintains a list of all available property editors (a property editor cannot be used until it is registered with the property editor manager).

The names of the editors are fairly self-explanatory. For example, the `BoolEditor` is used for boolean values, while the `ByteEditor` is used for byte values etc. Note that the colour editor is called `ColorEdit` after the American naming conventions.

Table 10.1: Property editors

| BoolEditor | ByteEditor | FontEditor | DoubleEditor |
|------------|------------|------------|--------------|
| ColorEditor | FloatEditor | StringEditor | IntEditor |
| NumberEditor | LongEditor | | |

Of course you are not limited to using these editors. You can define your own using the `PropertyEditor` interface or the `PropertyEditorSupport` class. These are described in the next two sections.

## The `PropertyEditor` Interface

In some situations you will want to define your own property editor. You can do this by implementing the `PropertyEditor` interface (for example the `ColorEditor` and the `FontEditor` both implement this interface). The methods defined by the `PropertyEditor` interface are presented in Table 10.2.

Table 10.2: The `PropertyEditor` interface methods

| Object getValue() | Returns the value of the property |
|-------------------|-----------------------------------|
| setValue(Object) | Set (or change) the object that is to be edited |
| String getAsText() | Returns the property value as a `String` |
| setAsText(String) | Set the property value by parsing a |

| | |
|---|---|
| | given `String` |
| `String getJavaInitialization-String()` | This method is intended for use when generating Java code to set the value of the property, for example `"new Color(127, 127, 127)"` or `"Color.red"` |
| `boolean isPaintable()` | Returns true if the property editor supports the `paintValue()` method |
| `paintValue(Graphics, Rectangle)` | Paint a representation of the value into a given area of screen real estate |
| `String[] getTags()` | If the property value must be one of a set of known tagged values, then this method should return an array of the tags |
| `Component getCustomEditor()` | A `PropertyEditor` may choose to make available a full custom `Component` that edits its property value |
| `boolean supportsCustomEditor()` | Returns `true` if the property editor provides a custom editor specified through a user-defined GUI |
| `addPropertyChangeListener( PropertyChangeListener)` | Register a listener for the `PropertyChange` event |
| `removePropertyChangeListener (PropertyChangeListener)` | Remove a listener for the `PropertyChange` event |

There are twelve methods specified by the `PropertyEditor` interface. You must implement them all. However, depending upon the type of editor you are defining some of the methods may return null. This indicates that they do nothing and thus all they should contain is the statement `return null`. For example:

```
public String [] getTags() {
  return null;
}
```

This would be used if the `PropertySelector` view were inappropriate. The PropertySheet expects a null parameter constructor to be provided by any editor class. Obviously a null constructor is provided by default if you have not provided any constructors yourself. However, if you provide one or more constructors (whether they have parameters or not) the default null parameter constructor no longer exists. Thus you must make sure that a null parameter constructor is available.

The key method in the `PropertyEditor` interface is the `setValue()` method. This method is used to modify a property of a bean. It is passed an `Object`. The method should then cast the object to the appropriate type and then set the property to this object. As an example, Listing 10.1 illustrates the steps performed.

### Listing 10.1: Modifying a property

```
private PropertyChangeSupport support =
                            new PropertyChangeSupport();
private String dayOfWeek;
public void setValue(Object object) {
   // Cast the object to the appropriate type#
   String s = (String)object;
   // Change the properties value
   changeDayOfWeek(s);
}
public void changeDayOfWeek(String day) {
   // Reset property
   dayOfWeek = day;
   // Change GUI representation
   ...
   // Inform listeners of change
   support.firePropertyChange("", null, null);
}
public void
addPropertyChangeListener(PropertyChangeListener l) {
  support.addProeprtyChangeListener(l);
}
public void
removePropertyChangeListener(PropertyChangeListener l) {
  support.removeProeprtyChangeListener(l);
}
```

The `PropertyChangeSupport` class (originally used with bound properties in Chapter 5) is used to inform the bean that a change should be made to its property. You may note that the `firePropertyChange()` method has a null property name and values. This may seem strange; however, it is a convention used to indicate that an (unspecified) change has taken place. It would have been good style for the JavaBeans developers to have provided a null parameter `firePropertyChange` method.

As you can see from the above example, and the previous descriptions, if you are implementing the `PropertyEditor` interface then you will need to:

- Define the methods specified in the interface (although some may do nothing except return null).
- Provide a null argument constructor.
- Support the addition and removal of `PropertyChange-Listeners`.

# The `PropertyEditorSupport` class

You do not need to implement the whole of the `PropertyEditor` interface. Instead you can extend the utility class `PropertyEditor-Support` (indeed you would normally extend the `PropertyEditorSupport` class rather than implement the `PropertyEditor` interface). As with other utility support classes this class merely provides null implementations for most of the methods in the `PropertyEditor` interface. As you have already seen, using the support classes can be much easier than working from scratch.

As suggested above, not all the methods defined by the `PropertyEditorSupport` are *null* implementations. In particular, the following methods are fully functional and may be used in subclasses:

- **public void setValue(Object)** This sets (or changes) the property being edited.
- **public Object getValue()** This returns the value of the property.
- **public boolean isPaintable()** Returns `false`.
- **public String getAsText()** Returns a string suitable for presentation to a human to edit or `null` if the value can't be expressed as a string.
- **public void setAsText(String)** Sets the property value by parsing a given `String`.
- **public boolean supportsCustomEditor()** Returns `false`.
- **public synchronized void addPropertyChangeListener( PropertyChangeListener)** Registers a listener for the `PropertyChange` event.
- **public synchronized void removePropertyChange-Listener(PropertyChangeListener)** Removes a listener for the `PropertyChange` event.
- **public void firePropertyChange()** Informs the listeners that the property has been modified.

As you can see from this list, the `PropertyEditorSupport` actually does a lot of work for you.

To give you some guidance on which to use, we have identified a number of rules:

- Use the `PropertyEditor` interface when you need a custom editor in a new window (see the source code for `FontEditor` and `ColorEditor` as examples).
- Use the `PropertyEditor` interface if you are extending an editor developed outside of the beans conventions.
- Use the utility support class when you only need to change a simple property editor that will be displayed within a property sheet (see the `BoolEditor` or `StringEditor` as examples).

The big advantage of using the `PropertyEditorSupport` class is that you only need to implement the relevant methods. For example, Listing 10.2 presents a property editor for the total property of the `monitor` bean. This property editor allows a user to specify only one of four time periods (10 seconds, 30 seconds, 1 minute or 2 minutes). As this is essentially a type of selection among alternatives, it implements the `getTags()` method and returns a string from the `getAsText()` method. This means that a choice box will be used by the PropertySelector view. This choice box will illustrate the four options (see Figure 10.3).

### Listing 10.2: The `TimeEditor` property editor

```
import java.beans.*;

public class TimeEditor extends PropertyEditorSupport {
    // Provides values for choice box
    public String[] getTags() {
        String result[] = { "2 minutes", "minute",
                            "30 seconds", "10 seconds" };
        return result;
    }

    // Converts the value passed in, into integers for
    // use by the associated bean property. We inherit
    // getAsText() from the parent class.
    public void setAsText(String text)
            throws java.lang.IllegalArgumentException {
        if (text.equals("minute")) {
            setValue(new Integer(60));
        } else if (text.equals("30 seconds")) {
            setValue(new Integer(30));
        } else if (text.equals("10 seconds")) {
            setValue(new Integer(10));
```

```
                   } else if (text.equals("2 minutes")) {
                        setValue(new Integer(120));
                   } else {
                        throw new java.lang.IllegalArgumentException(
                                                                 text);
                   }
              }
         }
         // Returns a string representing executable Java.
         public String getJavaInitializationString() {
              return getValue() + "";
         }
    }
```

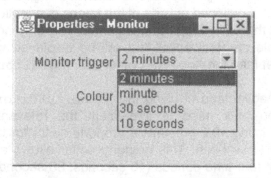

Figure 10.3: The `TimeEditor` choice box

# Registering a Property Editor

To register your property editor with the `PropertyEditorManager` you use the `getPropertyDescriptors()` method of the bean's `BeanInfo` (by setting the appropriate property descriptor object using the `setPropertyEditorClass()` method). If you do not do that, then you can call the editor *datatype*`Editor` and save it in the package directory of the bean or any other package on the `CLASSPATH`. Using the `BeanInfo` approach is cleaner and eliminates the chance of "picking up" the wrong *dataType*`Editor`.

Listing 10.3 present an example of how to do this. It adds the `TimeEditor` defined in Listing 10.2 to the property total of the `Monitor` bean.

**Listing 10.3: Adding the** `TimeEditor` **to the** `MonitorBeanInfo`

```
public class MonitorBeanInfo extends SimpleBeanInfo {
  private final static Class beanClass = Monitor.class;

  public PropertyDescriptor[] getPropertyDescriptors() {
    PropertyDescriptor total = null,
                        background = null;
    // Create a new PropertyDescriptor for MaxValue
    try {
      total = new PropertyDescriptor("total",
                                             beanClass);
      total.setDisplayName("Monitor trigger");

      total.setPropertyEditorClass(TimeEditor.class);

      background = new PropertyDescriptor("background",
                                             beanClass);
      background.setDisplayName("Colour");
    } catch (IntrospectionException e) {
      throw new Error(e.toString());
    }

    PropertyDescriptor result[] = { total, background };
    return result;
  }
  ...
}
```

The statement that adds the `TimeEditor` to the total property in Listing 10.3 is italicized to highlight it. As you can see all that is necessary is to use the `setPropertyEditorClass()` method to specify the actual editor class.

# Customizers

In some situations even defining your own property editor is not sufficient. In these situations customizers can be defined. These are similar to "wizards" in that they take the user through a series of decisions that have the combined effect of setting one or more properties in one go. Such a "wizard" is know as a customizer in JavaBeans.

All customizers must implement the `Customizer` interface (defined in the JavaBean API). This interface specifies three methods. These methods are:

`public void setObject(Object)` This method sets a reference to the object (bean) to be customized. This reference can be used elsewhere by the customizer to modify the beans properties etc. This method is only called once, before the Customizer has been added to any AWT container.

public void addPropertyChangeListener( Property-ChangeListener) This method records property change listeners.

public void removePropertyChangeListener( Property-ChangeListener) This method removes property change listeners from the customizer.

All customizers must also subclass the AWT Component class (or one of its subclasses). This is because the customizer will be displayed within a Dialog box. This means that it must be capable of being added to a AWT container. Any AWT component can be added to such containers. In general, you will subclass a container class such as Panel, which will allow you to create your own display within the Panel. This Panel will then be added to the Dialog window. This also means that all the facilities available in Java for creating graphical interfaces can be used to create a JavaBeans customizer.

The BeanBox (and other builder tools) will assume that a null parameter constructor is available from which to instantiate the customizer. It is therefore necessary to ensure that one is available. This can be done either by relying on the presence of the default constructor or by explicitly providing one. You should in general provide one of your own, as this is a more robust solution.

Once we have done all this we are in a position to make use of the customizer. To do this we need to inform the BeanInfo object that the customizer is available. If you look back at Chapter 7 you will note that it is the getBeanDescriptor() method which returns a BeanDescriptor. If you then study the specification of the BeanDescriptor class you will find that this class registers and provides a bean's customizer. In particular, it provides two constructors, one taking only a single argument (the bean being described) and a second taking two arguments (the bean being described and the bean's customizer). We therefore need to create an instance of a BeanDescriptor, passing to it the Class object for the appropriate customizer.

From the above description you should now be able to see that there are a number of steps required to create and use a customiser; these are:

- Extend java.awt.Component or one of its subclasses (such as Panel).

- Implement the `Customizer` interface.
- Provide a null argument constructor for the customizer.
- Define a `BeanInfo` file to specify the customizer, that is, define the `getBeanDescriptor()` method (see below).

Of course, customizers can also implement any event handlers required by the actual customizer as well as methods such as `getMinimumSize()` and `getPreferredSize()`.

As with everything in JavaBeans there is a naming convention associated with customizers. This convention is that the customizer will be called *BeanName*`Customizer`. Thus if we wished to define a customizer for the `Alarm` bean, it would be called `AlarmCustomizer`. One difference about this naming convention (compared to the other naming conventions in JavaBeans) is that it is only a convention – it is not enforced (at least not by the BeanBox tool).

The next section presents an example of defining a customizer for the `Alarm` bean used in the simple egg-timer application.

## The AlarmCustomizer

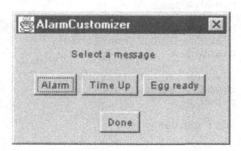

Figure 10.4: The Alarm bean customizer

We will use the `Alarm` bean as the basis of our example customizer. This customizer will display the window illustrated in Figure 10.4. This window allows a user to specify a message to be displayed by the Alarm without needing to know anything about how the bean is defined.

The definition of the `AlarmCustomizer` is presented in Listing 10.4. As you can see from this listing, this is a very simple customizer. However, a far more powerful customizer can be defined which will have the same essential structure as that presented.

### Listing 10.4: The `AlarmCustomizer` class

```java
import java.beans.*;
import java.awt.*;
import java.awt.event.*;

/**
 * Provides a customizer class for the Alarm bean.
 */
public class AlarmCustomizer extends Panel
                implements Customizer, ActionListener {
    private PropertyChangeSupport support =
                    new PropertyChangeSupport(this);
    private Alarm bean = null;

    /**
     * Null parameter constructor - required.
     * Sets up the customizer window components
     */
    public AlarmCustomizer() {
        setLayout(new BorderLayout());
        Panel p = new Panel();
        p.add(new Label("Select a message"));
        add("North", p);

        p = new Panel();
        Button b = new Button("Alarm");
        b.addActionListener(this);
        p.add(b);

        b = new Button("Time Up");
        b.addActionListener(this);
        p.add(b);

        b = new Button("Egg ready");
        b.addActionListener(this);
        p.add(b);

        add("Center", p);
    }

    public Dimension getPreferredSize() {
        return new Dimension(200, 70);
    }

    public void addPropertyChangeListener(
                        PropertyChangeListener l) {
        support.addPropertyChangeListener(l);
    }

    public void removePropertyChangeListener(
                        PropertyChangeListener l) {
        support.removePropertyChangeListener(l);
    }

    /**
     * Maintains a reference to the object to be
     * customized.
```

```
      */
     public void setObject(Object object) {
        bean = (Alarm)object;
     }

     /**
      * Called whenever one of the option buttons is
      * clicked. Sets the message on the bean and fires
      * the property support method FireProeprtyChange to
      * inform any listeners of the change.
      */
     public void actionPerformed(ActionEvent event) {
        String s = event.getActionCommand();
        bean.setMessage(s);
        support.firePropertyChange("message", "", "");
     }
  }
```

In order to be able to use this customizer class with the `Alarm` bean we need to define the `getBeanDescriptor()` method in the `AlarmBeanInfo` class. Listing 10.5 illustrates the result of adding the `getBeanDescriptor()` method.

### Listing 10.5: Linking the customizer class to the `Alarm` bean

```
import java.beans.*;
import java.awt.Image;
import java.lang.reflect.*;

public class AlarmBeanInfo extends SimpleBeanInfo {
    private final static Class beanClass = Alarm.class;

    public Image getIcon(int iconKind) {
       ...
    }

    public BeanDescriptor getBeanDescriptor() {
      return new BeanDescriptor(beanClass,
                                AlarmCustomizer.class);
    }

}
```

As you can see from this listing, essentially you need to create a `BeanDescriptor` class that takes two parameters: the bean class object and the customizer class object.

# 11 *JavaBeans and ActiveX*

## Introduction

This chapter very briefly introduces the JavaBeans/ActiveX bridge. This is provided as many developers of JavaBeans will want to be able to make their beans available to Microsoft-based applications. In general these applications can only exploit software components which following the ActiveX model. This bridge allows beans to be used in place of standard ActiveX components.

## Overview

On completion of this chapter you will be able to:

- Explain the ActiveX model.
- Describe the ActiveX bridge.
- Package a bean as an ActiveX component.

## The Component Object Model

The Component Object Model (COM) is Microsoft's attempt to solve the problems of software integration and development. That is, a developer can build software from component parts rather than from scratch (*à la* JavaBeans). COM provides a framework for creating and using software components. This framework involves controls, registers, interfaces and server objects. The actual software that is packaged as a component (and is called an object) can be implemented in any language (although it is typically implemented in C++). The intention is that a developer need not sacrifice performance, language choice or extensibility when using COM. Thus COM imposes very little restriction on the developer. In terms of the Microsoft world, the "object" can be provided as a DLL or an executable (.EXE) and be local or remote (via Distributed COM – DCOM).

The object itself does not need to be implemented in an object oriented language (indeed it is often implemented in C or Visual Basic). Rather, it is treated as a software object which has a published interface and responds to requests to execute functions (methods).

The key to accessing these functions is the interface. An interface includes the set of functions that are callable on the object (and that act as a "contract" between the component and the software which uses the component). That is, a component implementing an interface guarantees to implement all the functions listed in that interface. In addition, one object can implement multiple interfaces, allowing it to present different sets of functions depending upon its use. All COM objects implement the IUnknown interface (which is also the root interface of the interface hierarchy). This interface provides the QueryInterface function which allows software to obtain information on the COM objects' other interfaces. All the interfaces are defined in an Interface Definition Language (IDL) which is very similar to C++. In addition, interfaces can inherit from each other. The interfaces are compiled using Microsoft's IDL (MIDL) compiler.

The Type Library is the (D)COM repository of interfaces. It is used by clients to discover what interfaces an object supports and what parameters are needed to invoke a particular function. This therefore acts as a partial interface to the COM world from other software.

Another important element of COM is the registry. Entries in this provide the information necessary to create the COM objects. At run-time the COM ORB (object request broker) called the COM Run-time handles access to COM objects.

For more information on COM see Dale Rogerson, *Inside COM*, Microsoft Press, Redmond WA, 1-572-31349-8, 1996.

# What is ActiveX?

ActiveX is a marketing name for a set of technologies and services that are based on COM and DCOM. Essentially, an ActiveX component is a COM object packaged with additional control information. One of the limitations of the ActiveX model is that it does not work outside of the Win32 environment. That means that any ActiveX components cannot be used on anything but a PC running either Windows 95 or Windows NT. For many organizations this is not a problem. However, if you have a variety of platforms, then it may be a consideration. Another consideration is that ActiveX components require another application within which to execute. They cannot be treated as standalone programs. In contrast, there is no reason why a JavaBean should not be executed as a standalone program if appropriate (as long as a `public static void main(String [])` method has been defined for it).

# ActiveX Bridge

The JavaBeans Bridge for ActiveX provides a link between the JavaBeans world and the Microsoft ActiveX world. This means that ActiveX components can be embedded in JavaBeans applications and that JavaBeans can be embedded in Microsoft applications (such as Internet Explorer, Word or Visual Basic). These applications are termed ActiveX containers.

From the point of view of ActiveX users, they are not aware that they are getting anything other than an ActiveX component; thus they are completely insulated from the Java side of the bean. This means that JavaBean developers not only have the huge advantage of write once, run anywhere, they can also deliver JavaBeans as beans or as ActiveX components (whichever the user of the bean prefers).

So what does the JavaBeans Bridge for ActiveX provide? It contains a packager utility class, a mapping from beans events to ActiveX events and a link between beans and ActiveX method invocation (so that tools such as Visual Basic can call a bean's methods).

The packager is a graphical utility that helps the developer to create OLE type library information and Win32 registry information for beans. This allows the OLE/COM containers to correctly analyse and present a bean. For example, this ensures that a bean's properties will be correctly published and that a Visual Basic property sheet can display them.

The bridge therefore allows a bean to act as a source for OLE/COM events and as a server for OLE/COM method calls.

The JavaBeans/ActiveX bridge can be downloaded from Sun: see http://java.sun.com/beans/software/bridge.

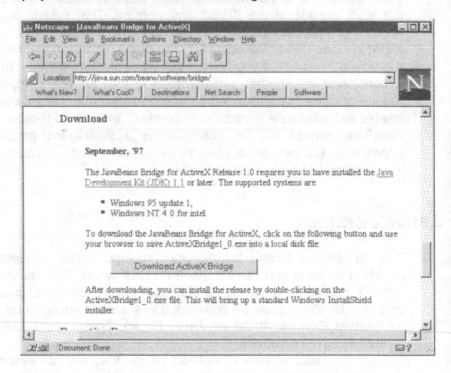

Figure 11.1: The ActiveX download web page

This presents a Web page (illustrated in Figure 11.1) with information about the current release of the ActiveX bridge as well as the ability to download a .exe program. You will need to specify what operating system you are using (Windows 95 or Windows NT). After downloading the .exe file, you can install the bridge by executing this installation program. The result is the addition of a new subdirectory to the BDK called bridge (illustrated in Figure 11.2).

# Packaging a bean

The packager takes a bean (held within a JAR file) and creates three outputs (as illustrated in Figure 11.3). These are the registry file, the

Java stub files and the Type Lib file. These are described in more detail below:

Figure 11.2: The `package` directory and subdirectories

- The registry file is created as an interim step. This file contains an object id, the executable path for the component, bridge information and a type library path.
- The Java stub files. Both `.java` source files and `.class` files are initially created (although the `.java` source files are deleted once the bean has been successfully wrapped up as an ActiveX component.
- The Type Lib file (which is a binary file) describes each component's properties, events and methods.

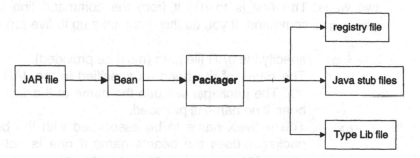

Figure 11.3: The packager's effect

Once the packaging process is complete the `.class` files are then
added to the JAR file containing the bean. The packaged bean can
then be used within any ActiveX container. The bean can also be
bundled with the Bridge run-time to be used as an ActiveX component
in environments which do not possess the full ActiveX bridge (see
Figure 11.12 for an example of using an `ExplicitButton` bean as
an ActiveX component within word).

## Creating an ActiveX component

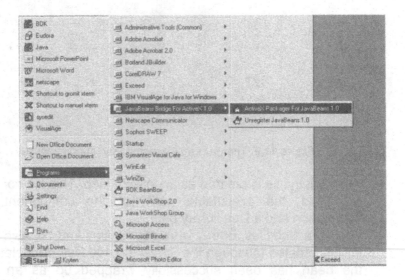

Figure 11.4: Starting the packager from the Start menu

This involves running the packager tool. This can be done in one of
two ways. The first is to run it from the command line using the
`packager` command. If you do this it can take up to five arguments:

| | |
|---|---|
| `-jar` | specify the JAR file path (must be provided). |
| `-n` | The name of the bean as specified in the JAR manifest file. The packager will use the name of the first available bean if no name is provided. |
| `-ax` | The ActiveX name to be associated with the bean. The packager uses the bean's name if one is not provided (minus the proceeding package names). |
| `-o` | The output directory for the type lib and registry files. |
| `-awt` | Specifies whether events should follow the AWT standard. |

As the packager executes it provides information on its progress to the standard output.

The second, often more convenient, way to run the packager is as a GUI application. This is done by selecting the packager from the **Start** menu. This is illustrated in Figure 11.4.

Having done this, you will be presented with the window illustrated in Figure 11.5. This acts as a "wizard" which takes you through five steps to package your bean. This first step involves specifying the JAR file which contains the bean. Once you have done this select **Next**. Note that you can browse your file store to select the appropriate JAR file using the **Browse** button.

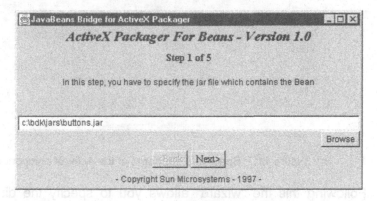

Figure 11.5: Starting the packager

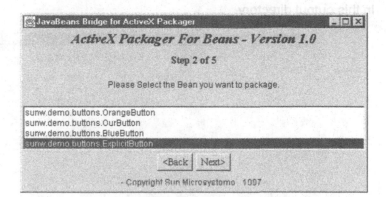

Figure 11.6: Selecting the bean to package

The screen you are presented with includes a selection list that presents all the beans in the specified JAR file. In the example in Figure 11.6 the beans in the buttons.jar file (provided with the

BDK) are listed. We have selected the `ExplicitButton` bean (used in the egg-timer application) and are ready to select **Next**.

If you realize at this point that you have selected the wrong JAR file, you can go back to the previous screen and select a different file using the **Back** button.

The next screen allows you to specify an ActiveX name for your bean. By default it is the (de-packaged) name of your bean. In Figure 11.7 we have called the ActiveX component JohnsButton.

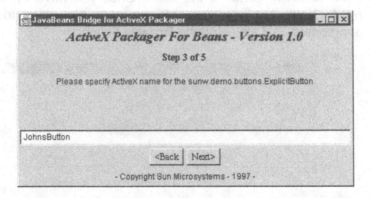

Figure 11.7: Specifying the name of the ActiveX component

Following this the "wizard" allows you to specify the directory into which the registry and type library files will be saved (see Figure 11.8). Note that it is assumed that the `beans.ocx` file is also located in this output directory.

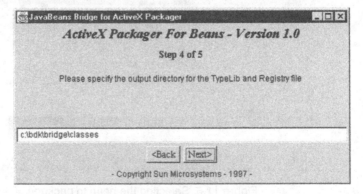

Figure 11.8: Specifying the save directory

The final window (Figure 11.9) allows you to specify whether the new ActiveX component should be registered immediately on the current machine. It also allows you to indicate the type of events to be generated. Essentially, cracked events are AWT type events while uncracked events are COM type events.

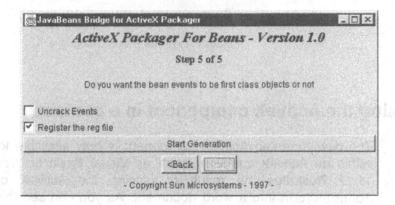

Figure 11.9: Starting the generation

You are now ready to start the generation process. Once you have done this, a new screen is displayed which provides progress messages from the packager. This is illustrated in Figure 11.10.

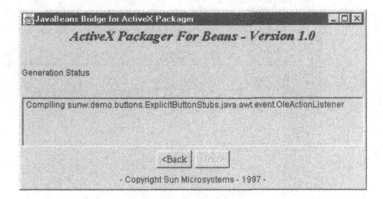

Figure 11.10: The packager progress window

Once the packager is finished it displays a status dialog (Figure 11.11) illustrating whether it was successful or not.

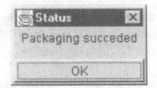

Figure 11.11: The status dialog

# Using the ActiveX component in a container

The newly created ActiveX component is now available to be used within an ActiveX container such as Visual Basic or Word. Figure 11.12 illustrates the result of placing the ActiveX component JohnsButton into a word document. As you can see this appears very similar to how it would appear as an ExplicitButton in the BeanBox.

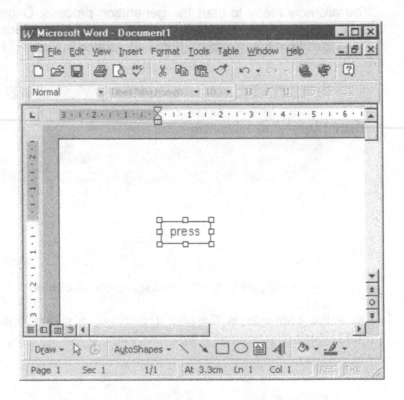

Figure 11.12: Adding a bean as an ActiveX control

To add an ActiveX control go to the **View** menu, and select the **Toolbars** option. Next select the **Control Toolbox** option. This brings up a select window. Next go to the **More Controls** option (in Word 97 it looks like a crossed hammer and spanner). You should now see a selection list similar to that in Figure 11.13. As you can see from this list, `JohnsButton` has been selected.

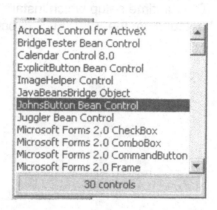

Figure 11.13: Selecting the ActiveX control

If you double click on this component you can bring up a set of windows which allow you to set the properties of this component, as well as what happens when the button is pressed (here you need to implement the `JohnsButton1_actionPerformed` subroutine!). This is illustrated in Figure 11.14.

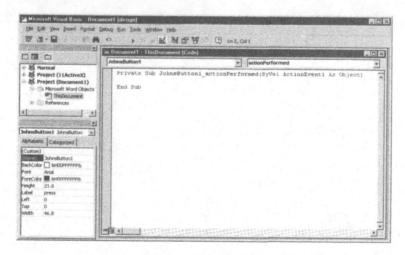

Figure 11.14: Setting the properties on the ActiveX component

# Run-time support

To distribute a packaged bean for a Windows application a run-time version of the JavaBeans Bridge for ActiveX is available (as part of the packager). By bundling the packaged JavaBeans and the Bridge Run-time, any Windows applications can act as an ActiveX container for the bean. The run-time setup which installs the run-time part of the bridge can be found in the `rtsetup` directory of the `packager` directory.

# *12* *Event*

## *Adapters*

## Introduction

This chapter introduces event adapters, what they are and how you use them. Event adapters are used to link event sources with event listeners in JavaBeans. This chapter explains this mechanism, as it is a necessary piece of knowledge if a developer is going to use JavaBeans outside builder tools such as the BeanBox.

## Objectives

Once you have finished this chapter you will be able to:

- Describe what an event adapter is.
- Explain the use of event adapters.
- Define an event adapter for a JavaBean.

## Event adapters

An event adapter is an object which sits between an event source and an event listener (as illustrated in Figure 12.1). It fills the gap between a bean which generates an event and a bean which responds to that event.

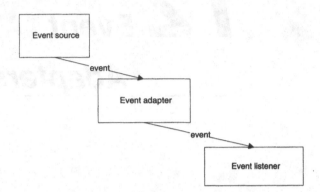

Figure 12.1: The role of an event adapter

Event adapters are not normally required in Java because the object which listens for an event directly implements the appropriate interface. It is then directly registered with the event source, so that the event source knows where to send the event. For example, let us assume that we are building some sort of graphical interface containing a button. Then we might define a button handler to deal with action events raised by a button:

```
public class ButtonHandler implements ActionListener {
  public void actionPerformed(ActionEvent e) {
    ... do relevant action
    }
}
```

We can now register instances of the ButtonHandler as the listeners of action events:

```
Button b = new Button("Load");
b.addActionListener(new ButtonHandler());
```

This is the normal way of creating objects which will handle events raised by components in the AWT.

However, if we examine the Clock class used in the egg-timer application constructed from the ExplicitButton, Clock, Monitor and Alarm beans, we note that it does not implement any listener interfaces. Yet the Clock bean can be registered as the event handler for an action event raised by the ExplicitButton bean. How is this possible?

The `Clock` bean can respond to events generated by the `ExplicitButton` bean because an event adapter sits between the two beans. This adapter catches the action event generated by the button bean. The adapter therefore implements the `ActionListener` and registers itself with the `ExplicitButton` bean as its listener. Within the adapter's `actionPerformed-(ActionEvent)` method, it then calls the method to be run on the `Clock` when the button is pressed. In the case of the egg-timer application, this is the `start()` method. Thus the `ExplicitButton` bean only knows about the adapter (which correctly implements the action listener). In turn the `Clock` is only aware of its `start()` method being directly called (it knows nothing about the event which initiated the execution of the method).

Why is this mechanism necessary? It is necessary because it would be impractical to expect a bean to implement every possible interface for all the events that it might need to respond to. Not only are there very many already, one of the purposes of the JavaBeans model is the ability to distribute beans. This means that it is impossible to know all the possible events any one bean may be subjected to. The adapter therefore provides the linking mechanism necessary to plug the gap.

## The use of Event adapters

When you link two beans together via the delegation event mechanism in JavaBeans an adapter class is automatically created for you. You may have noticed that an EventTargetDialog window pops up temporarily stating that the BeanBox is "Generating and compiling adaptor class" (for example see Figure 12.2).

The result is that whenever you use beans in this way an adapter class is always present. This means that if you try to use beans programmatically outside the BeanBox and want to connect them together in the way they were designed to be connected (that is, using the Delegation Event model) you will need to implement your own adapters. Of course the caveat on this is that, if the appropriate interface has been implemented, you do not need to use an adapter. However, as a bean may have been delivered to you without the source code, if it does not implement an appropriate interface then an adapter class is your only option.

Figure 12.2: Notifying the user of the creation of an adapter class

## Defining event adapters

Adapter classes are straightforward to define. They are normal classes which implement a specific interface. For example, if we wished to provide an adapter between the button bean and the `Clock` bean, then the adapter class must implement the `ActionListener`. Its `actionPerformed(ActionEvent)` method must call the `start()` method on the `Clock` bean. Listing 12.1 illustrates such an adapter class.

Listing 12.1: The `ActionEventAdapter` class

```
public class ActionEventAdapter implements ActionListener
{
    private Clock target = null;
    public ActionEventAdapter(Clock clock) {
    target = clock;
    }
    public void actionPerformed(ActionEvent event) {
    target.start();
    }
}
```

As you can see from this very simple example, there is nothing mysterious about adapter classes. It looks very much like any class which implements the `ActionListener` interface. The only difference is that it does not try to do anything with the `ActionEvent`; it merely calls the method `start()`.

Of course the `ActionEventAdapter` object must be registered with the `ExplicitButton` in the normal way using the `addActionListener()` method. For example:

```
Clock clock = new Clock();
ActionEventAdapter adapter = new
                          ActionEventAdapter(clock);
ExplicitButton b = new ExplicitButton("Start");
b.addActionListener(adapter);
```

In some cases an event adapter can be particularly useful as a multiplexer. This means that an event source sends one event to the adapter, but the adapter calls methods on multiple objects (the multiplexer can also send the event onto each object. This is illustrated in Figure 12.3 and Listing 12.2.

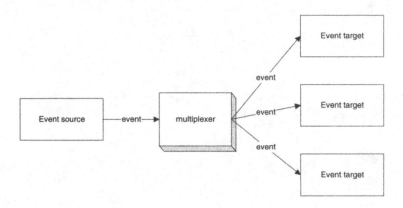

Figure 12.3: A multiplexing adapter

Listing 12.2: A multiplexing adapter

```
import java.util.*;
import java.awt.event.*;

public class Multiplexer implements ActionListener {
    private Vector targets = new Vector(10);
    public void addTarget(Object object) {
        targets.addElement(object);
    }
    public void removeTarget(Object object) {
        targets.removeElement(object);
```

```
    }
    public void actionPerformed(ActionEvent event) {
        ActionListener target;
        Enumeration enum = targets.elements();
        while (enum.hasMoreElements()) {
            target = (ActionListener)enum.nextElement();
            target.actionPerformed(event);
        }
    }
}
```

This can actually be a useful general technique for handling an event which must be sent to a number of objects without needing each object to register itself directly with the event source.

# 13

# RMI and Beans

## Introduction

All the beans you have considered in the last 12 chapters have been graphic beans. That is, they have a specific graphical display which is presented to the user in the BeanBox. However, in some situations there is no obvious graphical display for a bean. What happens then? This chapter presents a bean which allows a BeanBox application to connect to a server application. This bean does not have an inherent visual appearance, yet can still be created and manipulated within the BeanBox.

## Objectives

On completion of this chapter you will be able to:

- Define and manipulate non-graphical beans.
- Create an RMI server and client.
- Communication with remote objects using RMI.

# Non-graphical beans

As has already been stated, not all beans have a graphical representation. For example, a simple client bean which allows a user to connect to some server has no obvious display. It may well provide information to other beans which display this information, but it itself is non-graphical. However, all the beans we have defined so far have been subclasses of a graphic component (typically a subclass of Panel). However, if the client bean has no graphical representation it does not make sense to force it to have one. Indeed, conceptually it would be rather strange to have a client bean being a subclass of a Panel. However, if a bean has no representation how do we find it in the BeanBox, how do we manipulate it and how do we link it to other beans? The answer is that the BeanBox provide a graphical view of the bean during the build process.

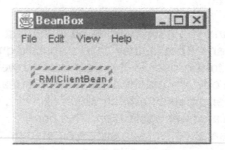

Figure 13.1: Displaying a non-graphical bean in the BeanBox

Figure 13.1 illustrates how the BeanBox displays the non-graphical bean RMIClientBean (described later in this chapter). Essentially it uses the name of the bean as the label to be displayed. It then allows the user to select the bean by clicking on the label. The BeanBox indicates that this bean is selected in the usual way using the hashed outline.

However, if the user does not wish to see the non-graphical beans their display can be turned off. This is done using the **View** menu. This menu includes a **Hide Invisible Beans** option (as illustrated in Figure 13.2). If the user selects this option the non-graphical beans will disappear. Note that the **View** menu option now changes to **Show Invisible Beans**.

Unlike beans with a graphical display, a non-graphical bean can inherit from an available class (apart from a graphic component as the BeanBox will then assume that it is a graphic bean!).

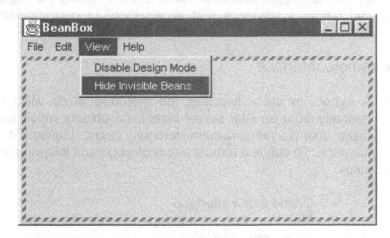

Figure 13.2: The **View** menu with **Hide Invisible Beans** selected

# Remote Method Invocation

Remote Method Invocation (or RMI) is one of the facilities provided in Java for implementing distributed systems (others include Sockets and interfaces to CORBA-compliant ORBs). RMI is similar in concept to Remote Procedure Calls (RPC) for procedural languages. Essentially, an object can invoke a method on another object in a separate process (potentially on a different machine).

RMI is surprisingly straightforward, merely requiring the developer to:

- define a remote interface (which specifies what methods are available remotely),
- subclass an appropriate RMI server class,
- run the rmic compiler on the server class to generate the stub and skeleton files used with RMI,
- register the remote object with the RMI registry.

The remote object is then available for use. In turn, the client need only obtain a reference to the remote object (via the registry) to be able to invoke remote methods on it. We will look at each of these steps in a little more detail.

Note that the registry is a central resource which records the names of remote objects and references to them. Using the registry clients can obtain a reference that allows them to communicate with the remote server.

## The remote interface

A remote interface specifies the methods which will be available remotely from an RMI server object. All objects which are going to make themselves available remotely must implement a remote interface. To define a remote interface you must following a number of steps:

- Define a new interface.
- Make this interface extend the interface `java.rmi.Remote`.
- Define any methods which are going to be available remotely (these methods must be `public`).
- Each method must declare that it throws the `java.rmi.RemoteException`.

As an example, consider the remote interface definition in Listing 13.1. This listing shows the `RMIBean` interface to be used by the `RMIClientBean`.

### Listing 13.1: The `RMIBean` remote interface

```
package rmibeans;

/**
 * The remote interface used to indicate which
 * methods are remotely available.
 */
public interface RMIBean extends java.rmi.Remote {
   public String query(String request)
                    throws java.rmi.RemoteException;
}
```

## Subclassing a server class

Once you have defined a remote interface you can now start to define the server class which implements this interface. To do this you need to:

- Specify the remote interface(s) being implemented by the server.
- Optionally subclass a remote server (e.g. `java.rmi.server.UnicastRemoteObject`).
- Provide implementations for the methods specified in the remote interface.
- Define a constructor for the server. This constructor must throw the `java.rmi.RemoteException`.
- Create and install the `java.rmi.RMISecurityManager`.

These steps sound complex, but are in reality straightforward. For example, Listing 13.2 illustrates the source code for the `RMIServer` remote object class. As you can see it implements the `RMIBean` interface and thus the `query(String)` method. It defines a null parameter constructor which throws the `RemoteException` exception (as indicated above). Within this constructor it first calls `super()`. This invokes the `null` argument constructor[1] of the `java.rmi.server.UnicastRemoteObject`. By doing this the remote object is "exported" so that it can handle calls to the remote object on an anonymous port (actually 1099). The constructor then uses the `setSecurityManager()` method of the `System` class to install a newly created instance of the `RMISecurityManager`. Note that we do not need to know much about this security manager to be able to use it.

### Listing 13.2: The `RMIServer` class

```
package rmibeans;

import java.rmi.*;
import java.rmi.server.UnicastRemoteObject;

/**
 * A RMI server bean. Used to connect the beans in one
 * BeanBox with other BeanBoxes. Receives a string which
```

---

[1] This would actually happen by default, but it is included here to indicate the operations occurring.

```
 * in this simple example merely returns Phoebe Hunt or
 * Unknown query.
 */
public class RMIServer extends UnicastRemoteObject
implements RMIBean {
    private String reply = "Phoebe Hunt";

    public RMIServer() throws RemoteException {
        super();
        try {
            System.setSecurityManager(
                                new RMISecurityManager());
            // Note hal.dcs.ac.uk is the name of the
            // server on which this RMIServer object is
            // running. RMI only lets it use the current
            // server.
            Naming.rebind("//hal.dcs.ac.uk/RMIServer",
                                                     this);
            System.out.println("RMIServer bound in
                                                 registry");
        } catch (Exception e) {
            System.out.println("RMIServer error " +
                                             e.getMessage());
            e.printStackTrace();
        }
    }

    public String query(String request)
            throws java.rmi.RemoteException {
        if (request.equals("Johns daughter"))
            return reply;
        else
            return "Unknown query";
    }

    /**
     * Test harness for RMIServer bean
     */
    public static void main(String args []) {
        try {
            new RMIServer();
        } catch (RemoteException e) {
            System.out.println("RMIServer error " +
                                             e.getMessage());
            e.printStackTrace();
        }
    }
}
```

The other thing to note is the call to `rebind()` sent to the class `Naming`. This is actually the process used to register this object with the RMI registry. This allows another object in a different process to obtain a reference to this object. Essentially the registry maintains a table of remote objects and how to reference them (i.e. the machine and port they are connected to). This process is illustrated in Figure 13.3.

Figure 13.3: How the registry manages RMI references

If you do not want to use the default port, a different port can be specified when the object is registered with the registry. For example, `//pcdhdc:1234/RMIServer` would connect the `RMIServer` to port 1234.

## Running the RMIC compiler

Once you have defined the server class and successfully compiled it, you can then run the `rmic` compiler. This compiler is applied to the `.class` file rather than the `.java` file. For example, to execute the rmic compiler on the `RMIServer` class just created we would issue the following command at the command line:

```
rmic rmibeans.RMIServer
```

Note that I have specified the package within which the `RMIServer` is implemented.This produces two additional `.class` files:

- `RMIServer_Skel.class`
- `RMIServer_Stub.class`

These files define the skeleton and stub files used to interface between the server and any clients. Essentially, the skeleton connects the server to the RMI framework, while the stub acts as a proxy server in the client's environment. This is illustrated in Figure 13.4.

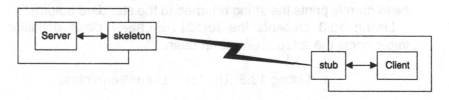

Figure 13.4: Using the skeleton and stub classes

## Starting the registry

We are now nearly ready to deploy our RMI server object. However, we must first start the RMI registry so that it can record the location and name of the server object. This is done by executing the `rmiregistry` command. This command produces no output and is typically run in the background. For example, on Windows95/NT you can issue the following command from the command line:

```
start rmiregistry
```

If `start` is not available you can use `javaw`.

The registry runs on port 1099 by default. If you want to start the registry on a different port, specify the port number in the command. For example, to run the registry on port 1234 use:

```
start rmiregistry 1234
```

You can now start the server object. As the `RMIServer` class implements the `main` method, this remote object can be initiated in the normal manner:

```
java RMIServer
```

## The `RMIClientBean`

As we now have a server object which is running and has registered itself with the RMI registry we can now create a client object. In our case we want to create a bean which will allow a set of beans to obtain information from the server (although in this case the client bean merely prints the string returned to the standard output).

Listing 13.3 presents the `RMIClientBean` class definition that implements the `RMIClientBean` bean.

Listing 13.3: The `RMIClientBean` class

```
package rmibeans;

import java.rmi.*;

/**
 * A simpel bean used to connecct to the
 * RMIServer remote object.
 */
```

```
public class RMIClientBean {
    private String question = "Johns daughter";
    public RMIClientBean() {
        try {
            // Gain access to the remote object.
            // Note hal.dcs.ac.uk is the name of the
            // server on which the RMI server object is
            // running.
            RMIBean remoteObject =
                (RMIBean)Naming.lookup(
                            "//hal.dcs.ac.uk/RMIServer");
            // Get string from remote object
            String reply = remoteObject.query(question);
            System.out.println(reply);
        } catch (Exception e) {
            System.out.println("RMIClientBean error " +
                                        e.getMessage());
            e.printStackTrace();
        }
    }
}
```

The RMIClientBean is an extremely simple bean, which possesses no properties but which obtains a reference to the RMIServer object using the following statement:

```
(RMIBean)Naming.lookup("//hal.dcs.ac.uk/RMIServer");
```

Note that it has to specify the machine on which the server is running as well as the name given to the server. Also note that the object returned by the `lookup` method needs to be cast to the remote interface type (in this case `RMIBean`). The resulting object can now be used in just the same way as a local object. In fact, it is a local object (the stub object). The calls are then passed onto the actual server object via the RMI framework.

# The manifest file

We now need to package our `RMIClientBean` so that the BeanBox can use it. This is done in exactly the same way as for any other bean (i.e. in a JAR file). In this case we must also include the `RMIBean` interface in the jar file so that the BeanBox can find it. Thus the manifest file for the `RMIClientBean` looks like that presented in Listing 13.4.

Listing 13.4: The manifest file

```
Name: rmibeans/RMIClientBean.class
```

```
Java-Bean: True

Name: rmibeans/RMIBean.class
Java-Bean: False
```

## Building the JAR file

To create the jar file we can use the `jar` tool as illustrated below:

```
jar cvfm c:\bdk\jars\rmibeans.jar rmibeans\manifest.tmp
rmibeans\*.class
```

## Using the RMI bean

The `RMIClientBean` will now appear in the ToolBox pallette of the BeanBox the next time it is run. This bean can now be used within the BeanBox in exactly the same way as any other bean. Of course, to allow you to pass queries to it from other beans it would need to be extended; however, that is left as a task for the reader. At present once you add it to the BeanBox, the `RMIClientBean` will connect to the `RMIServer` object and retrieve a string. This string will be displayed in the standard output.

# Appendix A: The `Clock` bean

## A.1 The `Clock.java` file

```java
import java.awt.*;
import java.awt.event.*;
import java.beans.*;

/**
 * Provides a real-time clock which can
 * be used with other beans that
 * require notification at specified intervals
 *
 */
public class Clock extends Panel implements Runnable{
    // Internal time
    private float time = 0.00f;
    private int interval = 1;
    private TextField field = new TextField(4);
    private Thread thread;
    private boolean running = false;
    // Bound property support
    private PropertyChangeSupport support =
                            new PropertyChangeSupport(this);

    /** Null parameter constructor used to create
      * instances of the clock
      */
    public Clock() {
        add(field);
        field.setText(time + "");
        thread = new Thread(this);
    }

    /**
     * Event listener registration method
     */
    public void addPropertyChangeListener(
                            PropertyChangeListener l) {
        support.addPropertyChangeListener(l);
    }
    /**
     * Event listener de-registration method
```

```
   */
  public void removePropertyChangeListener(
                              PropertyChangeListener l) {
     support.removePropertyChangeListener(l);
  }

  /**
    * sets the notification interval
    */
  public void setInterval(int i) {
     interval = i;
  }

  /**
    * Get the current interval used to notify of clock
    * ticks.
    *
    * @return int interval
    */
  public int getInterval() {
     return interval;
  }

  /**
    * Get the current time
    * @return float time
    */
  public float getTime() {
     return time;
  }

  /**
    * Set the current time
    */
  public void setTime(float f) {
     time = f;
  }

  /**
    * Start the clock ticking.
    */
  public void start() {
     if (!running) {
        thread.start();
        running = true;
     }
  }

  /**
    * Increments the time property. As this is
    * a bound property it notifies any beans
    * interested in this property of the change
    */
  public void increment () {
     float oldTime = time;
     time = time + interval;
     field.setText(time + "");
     support.firePropertyChange("time",
                                new Float(oldTime),
```

```
                                        new Float(time));
   }

   /**
    * Should not call directly - use the start() method
    */
   public void run() {
      try {
         thread.sleep(interval * 1000);
         while (true) {
            increment();
            thread.sleep(interval * 1000);
         }
      } catch (InterruptedException e) {}
   }

   /**
    * Test harness for the clock class
    */
   public static void main (String args []) {
      Clock c = new Clock();
      c.start();
   }
}
```

## A.2 The `ClockBeanInfo` file

```
import java.beans.*;
import java.awt.Image;
import java.lang.reflect.*;

/**
 * Provides the BeanInfo object for the Clock bean
 */
public class ClockBeanInfo extends SimpleBeanInfo {
   private final static Class beanClass = Clock.class;

   /**
    * Returns the specified type of image
    */
   public Image getIcon(int iconKind) {
      Image img = null;
      if (iconKind == BeanInfo.ICON_MONO_16x16 ||
         iconKind == BeanInfo.ICON_COLOR_16x16 ) {
         img = loadImage("Clock16.gif");
      } else if (iconKind == BeanInfo.ICON_MONO_32x32 ||
         iconKind == BeanInfo.ICON_COLOR_32x32 ) {
         img = loadImage("Clock32.gif");
      }
      return img;
   }

   /**
    * Returns an array of descriptors for the properties
    * of the Clock bean.
    */
```

```java
    public PropertyDescriptor[] getPropertyDescriptors() {
        PropertyDescriptor time = null, background = null,
                            interval = null;
        // Create a new PropertyDescriptor for MaxValue
        try {
            time = new PropertyDescriptor("time",
                                          beanClass);
            time.setDisplayName("Start Time");
            time.setBound(true);
            background = new PropertyDescriptor(
                            "background", beanClass);
            background.setDisplayName("Colour");
            interval = new PropertyDescriptor("interval",
                                          beanClass);
        } catch (IntrospectionException e) {
            throw new Error(e.toString());
        }

        PropertyDescriptor result[] = {time,
                                       background,
                                       interval };
        return result;
    }

    /**
     * returns and array of method descriptors for the
     * the method made publically available (actually only
     * start()).
     */
    public MethodDescriptor [] getMethodDescriptors() {
        // First find the "method" object.
        Method method = null;
        MethodDescriptor result[] = new MethodDescriptor[1];
        try {
            method = beanClass.getMethod("start", null);
            result[0] = new MethodDescriptor(method);
        } catch (Exception ex) {
        // "should never happen"
        throw new Error("Missing method: " + ex);
        }
        return result;
    }
}
```

# Appendix B: The Monitor Bean

## B.1 The Monitor.java file

```java
import java.beans.*;
import java.awt.*;
import java.util.*;

/**
 * This class provides a monitor facility for counting
 * property changes before triggering another bean.
 */
public class Monitor extends Panel
                     implements PropertyChangeListener {
    private long count = 0, total = 3;
    private Label label;
    private Vector listeners = new Vector(4, 4);
    public Monitor() {
        setBackground(Color.white);
        setForeground(Color.black);
        label = new Label(count + "");
        add(label);
    }
    public Dimension getMinimumSize() {
        return new Dimension(30, 30);
    }
    public Dimension getPreferredSize() {
        return new Dimension(30, 30);
    }
    public long getTotal() {
        return total;
    }
    public void setTotal(long t) {
        total = t;
    }
    /**
     * Handle property change events by calling
     * increment
     */
    public void propertyChange(
                        PropertyChangeEvent event) {
        increment();
    }
```

```
/**
 * Register a trigger event listener object
 */
public synchronized void addMonitorTriggerEventListener(
                    MonitorTriggerEventListener l) {
    listeners.addElement(l);
}
/**
 * De-register a trigger event listener object
 */
public synchronized void
                    removeMonitorTriggerEventListener(
                    MonitorTriggerEventListener l) {
    listeners.removeElement(l);
}
/**
 * Increments the internal counter until the
 * maximum value is reached - then raises an alarm
 * event.
 */
public void increment() {
    count++;
    if (count < total)
        label.setText(count + "");
    else {
        MonitorTriggerEvent mte =
                        new MonitorTriggerEvent(this,
                                            count);
        synchronized (this) {
            MonitorTriggerEventListener ml;
            Enumeration e = listeners.elements();
            while (e.hasMoreElements()) {
                ml = (MonitorTriggerEventListener)
                                    e.nextElement();
                ml.monitorTriggerEventHandler(mte);
            }
        }
    }
}
```

# B.2 The `MonitorBeanInfo` file

```
import java.beans.*;
import java.lang.reflect.*;

/**
 * Provides a BeanInfo object for the Monitor class.
 */
public class MonitorBeanInfo extends SimpleBeanInfo {
    private final static Class beanClass = Monitor.class;

    public PropertyDescriptor[] getPropertyDescriptors() {
        PropertyDescriptor total = null, background = null;
        // Create a new PropertyDescriptor for MaxValue
        try {
```

```java
            total = new PropertyDescriptor("total",
                                          beanClass);
            total.setDisplayName("Monitor trigger");
            background = new
                        PropertyDescriptor("background",
                                          beanClass);
            background.setDisplayName("Colour");
        } catch (IntrospectionException e) {
            throw new Error(e.toString());
        }

        PropertyDescriptor result[] = {total,
                                      background };
        return result;
    }

    public MethodDescriptor [] getMethodDescriptors() {
        // First find the "method" object.
        Method method = null;
        MethodDescriptor result[] = new MethodDescriptor[1];
        try {
            method = beanClass.getMethod("increment", null);
            result[0] = new MethodDescriptor(method);
        } catch (Exception ex) {
        // "should never happen"
        throw new Error("Missing method: " + ex);
        }
        return result;
    }

    /**
     * Returns an array of EventSetDescriptors indicating
     * the event to be raised by this class.
     */
    public EventSetDescriptor[] getEventSetDescriptors() {
        try {
            EventSetDescriptor monitor =
                new EventSetDescriptor(beanClass,
                        "monitorTriggerEventHandler",
                        MonitorTriggerEventListener.class,
                        "monitorTriggerEventHandler");

            monitor.setDisplayName("monitor triggered");

            EventSetDescriptor[] rv = { monitor };
            return rv;
        } catch (Exception e) {
            throw new Error(e.toString());
        }
    }
}
```

# B.3 The `MonitorTriggerEvent` file

```java
import java.util.EventObject;
```

```
public class MonitorTriggerEvent extends EventObject {
    long triggerValue = 0;
    public MonitorTriggerEvent(Object o,
                                        long triggeredValue) {
        super(o);
        setTrigger(triggeredValue);
    }
    public void setTrigger(long i) {
        triggerValue = i;
    }
    public long getTrigger() {
        return triggerValue;
    }
}
```

## B.4 The `MonitorTriggerEventListener` file

```
public interface MonitorTriggerEventListener {
    public void monitorTriggerEventHandler(
                            MonitorTriggerEvent event);
}
```

# Appendix C: The `Alarm` Bean

## C.1 The `Alarm` file

```java
import java.awt.*;
import java.awt.image.*;
import java.io.Serializable;

/**
 * Alarm bean class.
 * <p>
 * When triggered provides a warning
 * behaviour in a bean. This involves displaying
 * a specified image and message.
 */
public class Alarm extends Panel
                    implements MonitorTriggerEventListener,
                               ImageObserver,
                               Serializable {
    private boolean triggered = false;
    private String imageFile = "Alarm32.gif",
                   message = "Alarm";
    private Image image;
    public Alarm() {
        setBackground(Color.white);
        // Load the image to use with the alarm. This is
        // done in a platform independent manner using the
        // current toolkit.
        loadImage();
    }
    // This method uses the local toolkit to obtain an
    // image. Need to implement the ImageObserver interface
    // so that the progress of the image can be monitored
    // using the imageUpdate method (see below).
    private void loadImage() {
        try {
            Toolkit toolkit = Toolkit.getDefaultToolkit();
            image = toolkit.getImage(imageFile);
        } catch(Exception e) {
            System.out.println("Problem loading image");
        }
    }
```

```java
/**
 * Handler for the MonitorTriggerEvent
 */
public void monitorTriggerEventHandler(
                          MonitorTriggerEvent event){
    triggerAlarm();
}
/**
 * Indicates whether the alarm is triggered or not
 */
public boolean isTriggered() {
    return triggered;
}
/**
 * Used to set the message displayed with
 * the image when the alarm is triggered.
 */
public void setMessage(String message) {
    this.message = message;
}
/**
 * Used to get the message displayed with
 * the image when the alarm is triggered.
 */
public String getMessage() {
    return message;
}
/**
 * Used to set the image displayed with
 * the message when the alarm is triggered.
 */
public void setImageFile(String file) {
    imageFile = file;
    loadImage();
}
/**
 * Used to set the image displayed with
 * the message when the alarm is triggered.
 */
public String getImageFile() {
    return imageFile;
}
/**
 * Used when displaying the bean in the beanbox
 */
public Dimension getMinimumSize() {
    return new Dimension(60, 60);
}
/**
 * Used when displaying the bean in the beanbox
 */
public Dimension getPreferredSize() {
    return new Dimension(60, 60);
}
/**
 * Method used to cause the alarm to trigger
 */
public void triggerAlarm() {
    triggered = true;
```

```
      repaint();
   }
   /**
    * Used when displaying the bean in the beanbox
    */
   public void paint (Graphics gc) {
      if (isTriggered()) {
         gc.drawString(message, 5, 10);
         gc.drawImage(image, 10, 20, this);
      }
   }
   /**
    * Used while the image is loading
    * to determine if the image has
    * finsihed loading or not
    */
   public boolean imageUpdate(Image img,
                                        int infoflags,
                                        int x,
                                        int y,
                                        int width,
                                        int height) {

      if (ImageObserver.ALLBITS == infoflags)
         return false;
      else if (ImageObserver.ERROR == infoflags) {
      System.out.println("Error in image - image
                                      display aborted");
         return false;
      } else {
         return true;
      }
   }
}
```

## C.2 The `AlarmBeanInfo` object

```
import java.beans.*;
import java.awt.Image;
import java.lang.reflect.*;

/**
 * Provdies the BeanInfo object for the Alarm Bean.
 */
public class AlarmBeanInfo extends SimpleBeanInfo {
   private final static Class beanClass = Alarm.class;
   /**
    * Returns the icon to use in the ToolBox of the
    * bean box.
    */
   public Image getIcon(int iconKind) {
      Image img = null;
      if (iconKind == BeanInfo.ICON_MONO_16x16 ||
          iconKind == BeanInfo.ICON_COLOR_16x16 ) {
         img = loadImage("Alarm16.gif");
      } else if (iconKind == BeanInfo.ICON_MONO_32x32 ||
```

```
                        iconKind == BeanInfo.ICON_COLOR_32x32 ) {
                        img = loadImage("Alarm32.gif");
                }
            return img;
        }
    /**
     * Specifies the cutomizer to use with the
     * Alarm bean.
     */
    public BeanDescriptor getBeanDescriptor() {
        return new BeanDescriptor(beanClass,
AlarmCustomizer.class);
        }

}
```

## C.3 The `Alarm` Customizer

```
import java.beans.*;
import java.awt.*;
import java.awt.event.*;

/**
 * Provides a customizer class for the Alarm bean.
 */
public class AlarmCustomizer extends Panel
                    implements Customizer, ActionListener {
    private PropertyChangeSupport support =
                        new PropertyChangeSupport(this);
    private Alarm bean = null;

    /**
     * Null parameter constructor - required.
     * Sets up the customizer window components
     */
    public AlarmCustomizer() {
        setLayout(new BorderLayout());
        Panel p = new Panel();
        p.add(new Label("Select a message"));
        add("North", p);

        p = new Panel();
        Button b = new Button("Alarm");
        b.addActionListener(this);
        p.add(b);

        b = new Button("Time Up");
        b.addActionListener(this);
        p.add(b);

        b = new Button("Egg ready");
        b.addActionListener(this);
        p.add(b);

        add("Center", p);
    }
```

```java
    public Dimension getPreferredSize() {
        return new Dimension(200, 70);
    }

    public void addPropertyChangeListener(
                                PropertyChangeListener l) {
        support.addPropertyChangeListener(l);
    }

    public void removePropertyChangeListener(
                                PropertyChangeListener l) {
        support.removePropertyChangeListener(l);
    }

    /**
     * Maintains a reference to the object to be
     * customized.
     */
    public void setObject(Object object) {
        bean = (Alarm)object;
    }

    /**
     * Called whenever one of the option buttons is
     * clicked. Sets the message on the bean and fires
     * the property support method FirePropertyChange to
     * inform any listeners of the change.
     */
    public void actionPerformed(ActionEvent event) {
        String s = event.getActionCommand();
        bean.setMessage(s);
        support.firePropertyChange("message", "", "");
    }
}
```

# Appendix D: The Multiplexer

## D.1 The Multiplexer.java file

```java
import java.util.*;
import java.awt.event.*;

public class Multiplexer implements ActionListener {
    private Vector targets = new Vector(10);
    public void addTarget(Object object) {
     targets.addElement(object);
    }
    public void removeTarget(Object object) {
     targets.removeElement(object);
    }
    public void actionPerformed(ActionEvent event) {
     ActionListener target;
     Enumeration enum = targets.elements();
     while (enum.hasMoreElements()) {
        target = (ActionListener)enum.nextElement();
        target.actionPerformed(event);
     }
    }
}
```

# Appendix E: RMI Beans

## E.1 The `RMIBean` interface

```
package rmibeans;

/**
 * The remote interface used to indicate which
 * methods are remotely available.
 */
public interface RMIBean extends java.rmi.Remote {
    public String query(String request)
                            throws java.rmi.RemoteException;
}
```

## E.2 The `RMIServer` class

```
package rmibeans;

import java.rmi.*;
import java.rmi.server.UnicastRemoteObject;

/**
 * An RMI server bean. Used to connect the beans in one
 * bean box with other bean boxes. Receives a string which
 * in this simple example merely returns Phoebe Hunt or
 * Unknown query.
 */
public class RMIServer extends UnicastRemoteObject
implements RMIBean {
    private String reply = "Phoebe Hunt";

    public RMIServer() throws RemoteException {
        super();
        try {
            System.setSecurityManager(
                            new RMISecurityManager());
            Naming.rebind("//hal.aber.ac.uk/RMIServer", this);
            System.out.println("RMIServer bound in
                                            registry");
```

```
        } catch (Exception e) {
          System.out.println("RMIServer error " +
                                          e.getMessage());
          e.printStackTrace();
        }
    }

    public String query(String request)
              throws java.rmi.RemoteException {
      if (request.equals("Johns daughter"))
        return reply;
      else
        return "Unknown query";
    }

    /**
     * Test harness for RMIServer bean
     */
    public static void main(String args []) {
      try {
        new RMIServer();
      } catch (RemoteException e) {
        System.out.println("RMIServer error " +
                                          e.getMessage());
        e.printStackTrace();
      }
    }
}
```

## E.3 The `RMIClientBean` class

```
package rmibeans;

import java.rmi.*;

/**
 * A simple bean used to connect to the
 * RMIServer remote object.
 */
public class RMIClientBean {
    private String question = "Johns daughter";
    public RMIClientBean() {
        try {
            // Gain access to the remote object
            RMIBean remoteObject =

(RMIBean)Naming.lookup("//hal.aber.ac.uk/RMIServer");
            // Get string from remote object
            String reply = remoteObject.query(question);
            System.out.println(reply);
        } catch (Exception e) {
            System.out.println("RMIClientBean error " +
                                          e.getMessage());
            e.printStackTrace();
        }
    }
```

```
/**
 * Test harness for RMIClientBean
 */
public static void main(String args []) {
    new RMIClientBean();
}
}
```

## E.4 The `manifest.tmp` file

```
Name: rmibeans/RMIClientBean.class
Java-Bean: True

Name: rmibeans/RMIBean.class
Java-Bean: False
```

# Index

## A

ActionListener, 33
ActiveX, 4, 125
    Bridge, 9, 125
add/removePropertyChangeL
    istener(), 58
AdditionalInfo, 79
AdjustmentListener, 33
Alarm, 47, 102
AWT, 4, 29

## B

BDK, 3
Beans
       Graphical, 44
Beans/ActiveX packager, 126
BeanBox, 3, 6, 14
    JAR, 50
    Manifest, 50
    Starting, 14
BeanBox window, 16
BeanDescriptor, 72
Beans Development Ki, 3
Beans Development Kit
    obtaining, 9
Bean Info object, 41, 44, 68
BeanInfo interface, 42
BeanInfo, 72
    getAdditionalBeanInfo(), 80
    getPropertyDescriptors(), 73
Bean methods, 44
**Bind property...**, 56, 95
Bound property, 56

## C

Class.forName(String), 66,
    82
Class
    ObjectInputStream, 101
    ObjectOutputStream, 101
Clock **bean**, 86
ClockBeanInfo, 89
COM, 123
ComponentEvent, 33
ComponentListener, 33
Component Object Model, 123
Constructor, 66
Conventions, 42
Counter **bean**, 45
    Counter.ser, 69
    CounterCustomizer, 119
Constrained property 63
    SquareVetoer, 64
**Customize**, 23, 24, 109

## D

DCOM, 124
Delegation Event Model, 29
**Disable Design Mode**, 20
Duke, 27

## E

**Edit**, 19
    **Bind Property**, 57
    **Events**, 25
    **Report**, 69
    **Customize...**, 109

Egg timer application, 6
Event adapter, 135
     multiplexer, 139
Event classes, 37
Event Containment Hierarchy, 30
Event listener, 32
EventSetDescriptor, 72
ExitButtonHandler, 34
ExplicitButton, 24, 58
Externalizable interface,
     104

**F**

FeatureDescriptor, 72
Field, 66
**File**, 16, 18
    LoadJar, 28

**G**

getIcon(int), 90
getMethod(String,
    Class[]), 67
getMethods()        throws
    SecurityException,
    67
getSource(), 31

**H**

Help, 20
**Hide Invisible Beans**, 142

**I**

IndexedPropertyDescriptor
  , 72
ItemListener, 33
interface
    Serializable, 100
Introspection, 67
IntrospectionException, 72

**J**

JAR, 15
Java Development Kit
    obtaining, 8
java.awt.Component, 5
java.beans **package**, 5, 60, 71
java.beans.Beans.instanti
    ate(), 68
java.beans.PropertyEditor
    Manager, 111
java.lang.Class, 66, 67
java.lang.ClassNotFoundEx
    ception, 66
java.lang.reflect, 66
java.lang.reflect **package**,
    67
java.rmi.Remote, 144
java.rmi.RemoteException,
    144
java.rmi.RMISecurityManag
    er, 145
java.rmi.server.UnicastRe
    moteObject, 145
java.util.EventObject, 49
java.util.TooManyListener
    s-Exception, 40
JavaBeans, 3
   Alarm **bean**, 49
   BeanInfo, 42, 79
   bound property, 58
   constrained property, 62
   Counter **bean**, 48
   customizers, 117
   Events, 6
   Event handling, 44
   firePropertyChange(),
     58
   fireVetoableChange(),
     63
   getbeanInfo(), 68

getBeanInfo(), 67
indexed property, 64
Introspection, 67
introspector, 67
Methods, 6
Properties, 5
PropertyCanvas, 108
PropertyChangeEvent, 62
PropertyChangeSupport, 58
PropertyEditor, 114
PropertyEditorManager, 116
PropertyEditorSupport, 114
PropertySelector, 108
PropertyText, 109
PropertyVetoException, 62
Serialization, 99
SimpleBeanInfo, 45, 79
Using beans, 51
VetoableChangeListener, 62
VetoableChangeSupport, 62
vetoablePropertyChange(), 62
JavaBeans/ActiveX bridge, 126
JBuilder, 28
JDBC API, 4

**K**
KeyListener, 34

**L**
Live Connect, 4
Live Object, 4

**M**
Manifest file, 82, 97

MaxValueListener, 47
Method, 66
Monitor bean, 38
MonitorEvent, 37
MonitorEventListener, 38
monitorEventPerformed(MonitorEvent), 38
MouseListener, 34
MouseMotionListener, 34
Multicast events, 40

**N**
Naming.rebind(), 146

**O**
Object
    saving to a file, 100
    serialization, 100
ObjectInputStream class, 101, 102
ObjectOutputStream class, 101
OCX, 4
OLE, 125

**P**
Persistent data, 100
Properties, 43
propertyChange(), 58
PropertyChangeEvent, 58, 72
PropertyChangeListener, 58, 72
PropertyChangeSupport, 72
PropertyDescriptor, 72, 80
Property editors, 111
PropertyEditor interface, 111
PropertyEditorSupport, 109, 111
PropertyNameDialog, 57
PropertySelector, 112

PropertySheet, 14, 108
PropertyVetoException, 72

## R

Reflection
    BeanInfo objects, 66
Remote Method Invocation, 143
RMI, 143
    Naming.rebind(), 146
    remote interface, 144
RMIBean, 144
rmic compiler, 147
RMIClientBean, 144, 148
rmiregistry, 148
Run-time
    ActiveX bridge, 134

## S

Saving object information, 100
Serializable    interface,
    104
serialization, 100
Serialization
    JavaBeans, 99

SerializeComponent, 104
Simple properties, 55
SimpleBeanInfo, 72, 79

## T

TextListener, 34
ToolBox, 14
ToolBox palette, 15
toString(), 31

## U

Unicast events, 40

## V

VBX, 4
VCL, 4, 41
VetoableChangeListener, 72
VetoableChangeSupport, 72
View, 19
Visual Café, 28
VisualAge, 28

## W

WindowEvent, 33
WindowListener, 33
Word, 132